The Golden Key
to Continuous Prosperity
How to Vote Yourself a Tax Break
(Without Any Reduction in Government Revenue)

by
Steven B. Cord
(Professor-Emeritus, I.U.P., and Executive Director,
The Center for a Better Economy)

authorHOUSE™

1663 LIBERTY DRIVE, SUITE 200
BLOOMINGTON, INDIANA 47403
(800) 839-8640
WWW.AUTHORHOUSE.COM

First published by AuthorHouse 02/07/05

ISBN: 1-4208-3315-4 (e)
ISBN: 1-4208-2904-1 (sc)

Library of Congress Control Number: 2005900683

Printed in the United States of America
Bloomington, Indiana

This book is printed on acid-free paper.

Table of Contents

*How a Simple Reform
Can Transform the World*

The simple no-cost proposal described in this book can do these things:

(1) It can lower taxes for most people without diminishing government revenue

(2) It can increase total wealth production.

If adopted for the entire economy, it could ensure continuous prosperity for all and end involuntary poverty and unemployment. If it isn't adopted, free enterprise and democracy will fade away. These are huge claims, but the reader is asked to suspend judgment until all the evidence is seen.

Writes book editor Terry A. Fye: "Every effort has been made to make The Golden Key to Continuous Prosperity easily read and understood. It is conversational in tone and has been written simply and clearly."

A Tax That Creates Jobs

The proposal described in this book is simple enough:

**Replace All Taxes on Income, Wages and Sales
With a Tax on the Annual Rent of Land**

In bumper-sticker format: land tax good, all other taxes bad. Or you might prefer – tax locations, not things produced. *This book will show you how a simple change in the law can greatly increase your net income.* The proposal advocated in this book can ensure prosperity for all and end involuntary poverty and unemployment.

Let's be perfectly clear about "land tax good" – the revenue from it is nice (sort of a bonus) but if it were thrown away or burned up in a huge annual bonfire on the White House lawn (or wherever) the economy would still greatly prosper. Of course, better uses can be found for the revenue, like reducing taxes on wages or sales.

Let's not tax what people produce, let's tax land instead.

Has this proposal already been tried? **Yes, many times, and _all_ empirical (factual) studies of these applications show a much-improved economy.** See chapter three. In fact, as we will see, the long-run continuance of democracy depends on it.

If jobs aren't taxed, won't there be more jobs? If we don't tax what people produce, won't the prices of produced things be lower? Won't involuntary poverty be eliminated? Cannot this tax lay claim to being the most important idea in the world's history? In comparison, isn't every other attempt at social improvement like rearranging the deck chairs on the *Titanic?*

It's important that we reduce or replace taxes on jobs and produced things with another source of governmental revenue. This book will show how that can be done.

But don't believe any of these claims until you see their ethical justification and factual substantiation; read on, then judge. This book will be presenting ample logic and evidence, but we can't do everything at once.

This all sounds almost too good to be true – but remember, *it has been tried on a small scale many times and has <u>always</u> succeeded.* Chapter three will present some of the factual support in easy-to-read form and you can get brief summaries of 215 more empirical studies (preferably by email) and there are many more such studies! Do you require any more factual proof?

The explanation starts with our treatment of land, of nature.

How The Proposal Works

Every land parcel can be rented out annually, and it is this potential annual rent, even if is not actually collected by landowners, that should be taxed, replacing as many other taxes as possible.

Important: do *not* merge land rent into the sale price of the building on it – these entities are entirely different and should be taxed differently. Land-rent income is clearly *actual* when the landrentowner and the improvement owner are different people, but when they are the same, as it is for most homeowners, the annual land-rent income is *imputed* - it exists even if it doesn't actually change hands. The land's sale price is based on it.

We are currently taxing land rent by taxing the land's sales price, but eventually we should tax the annual land-rent income directly (and not the value of the building on it). If a land tax replaces other taxes, most people will save because they have little taxable land income.

Even vacant lots have an annual rent, which is why they can be extremely valuable. The annual rent is based on the land's highest-and-best potential use (as permitted by zoning) and not at all on its current use.

This book does *not* advocate a higher tax on vacant land than on built-upon land. That's a terrible idea. Rather it advocates a higher tax on *all* land rent, whether the land is built upon or vacant, instead of on buildings or other human-produced goods and services.

This higher tax on land rent is hereafter referred to as LRT. It can *gradually* replace such harmful and regressive taxes as the local property tax on buildings or the federal tax on payrolls.

Since one tax will replace other taxes, government revenue will not be diminished. Most people will get tax reductions because they have little land rent income, actual or imputed, but are hit hard by taxes on what they produce. You will be one of the savers unless a significant portion of your income comes from land ownership (but even then, you would benefit from a production-tax-free economy).

Lower taxes on things you produce while the government gets the revenue it needs - can you support that? This book will even propose a way for *all* wage earners to get take-home pay increases.

Consider this: every American's share of the national debt, as of 12/04, was $24,510 (source: Heartland Institute), probably more now. Then add to that each American's share of federal taxes, as well as the taxes and deficits of localities and states: *the total exceeds what the average American earns yearly!* Then multiply all this by four to see how the typical American family would be affected.

The largest single expense of an average lifetime is taxes, especially for those high up on the career ladder. Many Americans won't have enough money for their entire retirement. We won't be able to pay for social-security privatization unless we tax land values or rent. We are gradually becoming socialized as we increasingly tax labor & capital. The situation is worse in most other countries - but this book will show how this burden can be lifted.

Many people, hearing this for the first time, worry about the approximately 1% of the American workforce that owns farmland, but surprisingly even they will benefit, too. To find out how, read chapter four.

Can LRT be a Single Tax – i.e., the only tax? Surprisingly yes; we could actually abolish all taxes on wages and investments and have more than enough revenue to run a government, but let us leave this important matter for later. For now, we need only consider what happens when we tax land values or rent enough to down-tax labor & capital.

How You Could Benefit

Here are some ways by which you could benefit from this proposal:

> It could reduce your taxes as well as the prices of what you produce or buy, without reducing government revenues

> Producers won't have to pay non-producers for the privilege of producing as land prices gradually decline

> It is the only way to contain urban sprawl into the clean-and-green countryside; that's why it's been called the environmentally "smart tax"

> Establishing democracy in the Middle East can defeat terrorism, but only LRT can provide the prosperity needed for democracy to succeed there

This book will fully explain these claims. Where this proposal has been applied it has already done these things to the extent attempted (though not yet the last benefit listed above).

I myself have done 18 empirical studies of actual LRT applications; measurable construction and renovation growth always resulted. Whenever possible, I compared the land-taxing cities to their neighbors - they always out-constructed and out-renovated them. You can't do better than 18 out of 18. Logical expectations have always been completely realized. I have encountered absolutely no contradicting *empirical* studies.

Shouldn't we all have equal access to the opportunities offered by nature? This requires either public landownership (highly impractical) or better, private landownership coupled with the tax-sharing of the land's benefits to everyone. Then we needn't tax-violate the private property rights of workers and investors.

The taxation of what you produce forces you to share your property with others. Yes, you are similarly appropriating the labor and property of others when they are taxed and you enjoy the

x

benefits therefrom – but mutual robbery is no way to run a society. This book offers an alternative.

Not unimportant: the reduction of taxes on labor & capital will increase the taxable annual rent of land, which in turn will enable the further reduction of taxes on labor & capital. Everyone will benefit, but particularly tenants, consumers, and the poor.

Tenants will eventually get rent reductions and consumers will eventually get lower prices because in the long run LRT is never passed on to them as either higher rent or higher prices (read any basic economics textbook on this). On the other hand, taxes on production are surely passed on to them.

All taxes yield governmental revenue, but in every other respect taxes on land rent are *completely the opposite* of taxes on labor & capital. That's because land is not produced by people whereas labor & capital are.

It should come as no surprise to you that there are literally hundreds, really thousands, of well-known endorsers of this proposal (FDR, TR, Churchill, John Dewey, ULI, eight American winners of the Nobel Prize in economics, etc.). They know – you can.

This could be heavy stuff to explain, but every effort has been made for easy and pleasant reading. Heavy subject, light treatment.

If It's So Good, Why Isn't It More Widespread?

This question is considered in considerable detail later in the book, but it naturally occurs to every reader and so ought to be considered now, if only cursorily.

In the first place, it *is* being much practiced in the world, but not as a Single Tax and not much in America. Those 237+ empirical studies were not done on Mars.

Secondly, the idea has been associated with Henry George, its 19th century explicator, but unfortunately it has been his incorrect theories that have been emphasized and not his correct ones – more about this later.

Thirdly, George's followers have urged the immediate universal adoption of LRT but have not adequately examined how to gradually implement it in the foreseeable future. However, after reading this book, you will know how to implement it.

Fourthly, Americans have become accustomed to suffering from taxes. "Nothing is inevitable except death and taxes," good old Ben Franklin intoned. But the proper taxes can greatly help us.

If you think there could be an alternative to tax suffering, read on. If you have abandoned hope, quit now.

"It Sounds Too Good To Be True!"

There's an old saying, "If a proposal sounds too good to be true, then it isn't true." Well, surely such a proposal demands careful checking. Is it fully logical? Is there factual evidence for it? These are the acid tests of truth. Let's hope this book meets those tests. This is what it claims to achieve:

- ✓ Continuous prosperity for all (but especially for the poor and unemployed)
- ✓ Lower taxes for most readers of this book (with absolutely no reduction in government revenues)
- ✓ The *only* way to ensure the long-run existence of free enterprise and democracy.

Numerous authors have claimed they have the answer to society's ills, but their prose has been dense and their claims inadequately substantiated. But this book has been written with crystal clarity for the average reader, and the proposal it advances has been endorsed by literally hundreds of well-known authorities. *Above all, it has worked <u>every</u> time it has been tried.*

Determine if the factual substantiation is fully adequate. In view of the failed social nostrums of many previous authors, it is wise to proceed carefully and rationally, but don't reject vast claims out-of-hand.

Be open to new ideas, but insist on logic and hard evidence. Don't be satisfied with the mindless quip, "if it sounds too good to be true, it isn't true."

I have made a special effort to obtain the opinions of many people on matters related to continuous economic prosperity for all. I am indebted to all of them. This book would have suffered without their input.

1

My experience has been that few people fully understand land rent taxation, so this chapter explains it carefully. It is divided into ten separate sections:

1. What land rent taxation is and is not
2. Five ways to implement it locally
3. How natural resource land-rent taxation is to be implemented
4. How localities would be affected
5. How the state and federal governments would be affected
6. How land prices would be affected
7. Is it liberal or conservative?
8. Fourteen differences between the land value tax and all other taxes
9. It is an ability-to-pay tax.
10. If all this is true, the long-run continuance of free enterprise and democracy becomes possible.

Chapter **1**

The Proposal

Mention the taxation of land rent to the average person and you're liable to hear, "why tax land – it produces no income. At least the building on it produces an income, so tax it."

No – why tax-penalize productive effort if we don't have to? Since no one produced land, a tax on it can't penalize production.

If we tax land values, we won't have any less land, will we? The earth won't shrink if it is taxed. But if we tax produced things (like buildings), we'll have less of them and they'll cost more.

I've heard it said, "My town has no land." But how can that be – is it built on a cloud? It turns out that the people who say this think of land as part of the building on it and only count vacant lots and farmland as land. But the land under buildings has a separate rental value that can be very high if its location is desirable.

Most people are familiar with the three prime laws of real estate value: "location, location, and location," but they don't apply these laws to tax policy. There is ample logical and empirical support for taxing land rent rather than produced things. But let's clear up certain preliminaries first.

If you tax buildings less, wouldn't you have more of them, and aren't they more likely to be renovated? And if you up-tax land rent to recoup the revenue lost by not taxing buildings so much, land-sites would have to be used more efficiently - otherwise, there'd be too much expense covered by too little income. And as with buildings, so with anything produced by human labor.

Don't be surprised that the facts completely support these expectations and explain why LRT has been endorsed by literally hundreds of well-known politicians and experts. Nonetheless, most people have not heard of LRT. They suffer from the taxation of labor & capital, but they are resigned to suffering.

Many wives, for instance, make little more than the minimum wage after taxes are deducted, yet they continue to work anyway (feminists arise - you have nothing to lose but the taxes on your labor – not only women's labor but men's also).

If we don't abolish poverty and unemployment by implementing LRT, these problems will get worse and our free economy and democracy will eventually fade away; this book will present logic and facts to support this vast claim. Isn't it economic insanity to try to eradicate poverty by subsidizing it with government programs and then tax-penalizing wealth-making in order to do so?

Claiming that LRT can remedy social ills may seem wild and chimerical now, but please withhold judgment until you have seen all the relevant facts.

What Land Rent Is

Land rent is location value, expressed monetarily. Don't thoughtlessly merge it into building value. Land has an annual rental income, either imputed (assumed) as when the improvement owner and the landowner are one and the same, or actually collected. Where the location is desirable, its annual rental and therefore sale price can be very high. Don't overlook land (except visually).

Everyone realizes that a vacant lot can command a high price, even though it currently has no income. It's not the current use that determines land price but the *potential* highest and best use in the foreseeable future (as limited by zoning). The more the potential annual rental income, the higher the sale price.

It is instructive to compare this distinction between land price and land rent income to a bank account. Suppose you have a bank account worth $10,000. It might yield $500/yr. interest income, in which case it can be sold for either $10,000 or for $500/yr. a year. We can use the same approach with a land investment except that its annual rent income is likely to be closer to $1,000/yr. because you are taking a greater risk.

The better locations (those commanding a higher land rent) are near shopping, jobs, government-provided services, a better climate or view, etc. As for farming, soil fertility is important - though these days, farmland is only a small part of total land value.

We can't emphasize enough that land values are completely separate from improvement values even though the same property-tax rate might apply to both. Two real-estate parcels with the exact same improvements will have different prices if one location is worth more than the other.

The potential land rent, not the current land rent, determines the sale price of the land parcel, which is completely separate from house value. The revenue of the property tax is equal to the rate (a percentage set by the city council, school board, etc.) times the total of all the locality's assessments.

Land prices can be well known. Government assessors are constantly assessing the market price of each property's land. They mimic the free market; in no way do they levy the property tax to be paid. Business people are buying and selling land all the time. Only real-estate neophytes think land values can only be guessed at.

Did you know that many states list your property's land and building assessments on the Internet? You shouldn't complain about your land assessment being listed (after all, it was made by God or nature) but isn't it an invasion of your privacy to have your building assessment information on view for everyone to see? Isn't that an unwarranted invasion of your privacy?

We shouldn't be concerned about the size of land-sites because the proposed tax is on price, not size. Farms are usually many acres in size but the value of each farm acre is usually quite low as compared to an urban acre; surprisingly, farmers would actually benefit from LRT, as will be made clear in a later chapter.

The appendix contains specific land-assessing procedures. Incidentally, don't be afraid of the Appendix; there are no alligators or other dangers in it. It deals mostly with LRT implementation and isn't difficult to understand.

If a valuable site is vacant or under-used, it un-knits the city. People have to walk or drive past it to get where they're going. Commuting times are lengthened, as are telephone wires, sewers, roads, etc. Total land values suffer. Only LRT can remedy this situation.

It is possible to alleviate the impact of the property tax on the poor, elderly and temporarily unemployed, especially if it is only on land. These alleviations are listed in the appendix.

Five Local LRT Methods

The local property tax is used not only by cities but also by counties and special-purpose districts. Especially important are school districts, which now levy a very high property tax and so especially should use LRT. There are six ways for any locality to gradually shift its property tax from buildings to land:

1) <u>Obey the law</u>, which almost everywhere maintains that land and buildings should be assessed at the same ratio to market value. Nevertheless, land is generally more under-assessed than buildings vis-à-vis market value. Requiring the current law to be obeyed would result in a building-to-land property-tax shift.

2) <u>Legally assess land closer to market value than buildings</u>. This would certainly result in a tax shift from buildings to land.

3) <u>Tax-exempt improvement assessments in whole or in part.</u> Such an exemption could either be a percentage or a dollar amount (dollar exemptions would give poor homeowners greater tax relief). It would give most voters significant tax reductions because they invest more in their building than in their land; isn't that true for you? It certainly is for poor people.

4) <u>Establish a separate tax on land only</u> to be earmarked for such popular projects as parks and highways. This would be in addition

to the already-existing property tax. Similarly, deficits could be met by a surtax on land assessments.

5) <u>Set a lower property-tax rate (a percentage) on building assessments than on land assessments</u> (the so-called two-rate property tax) instead of taxing both types of assessments at the same percentage rate. This will shift taxes from buildings to land. Taxing building assessments at the same rate as land assessments is like shooting yourself in the foot.

You could annually reduce the tax rate on building assessments until it reaches 0%. Experience suggests no more than a 20% property-tax rate reduction of the one-rate tax on buildings (but the reduction could be more if the property-tax rate is already low or if in ensuing years the voters become accustomed to the land-tax increases).

In other words, whatever revenue is lost by not taxing buildings so much is made up by taxing land assessments at a higher *rate*. In this way, the government neither gains nor loses revenue. Other taxes can also be reduced or eliminated. The appendix shows how to exactly compute the two property-tax rates.

It is absolutely imperative to suggest the two rates to city councils, school boards, etc. *prior* to meeting with them. To do this, examine the assessment records beforehand.

To find out how, see the appendix.

How Localities Would Be Affected

Localities – cities, counties, schools and other special districts – should realize that their local property tax is both good and bad because it is really two taxes in one: a tax on buildings (bad) and a tax on land (good). The appendix tells how to easily and quickly determine which taxpayers will save with a building-to-land tax shift *before* going public with the idea.

Not only would most property owners get tax reductions with a building-to-land-tax shift, but <u>all</u> tenants as tenants would eventually get space-rent reductions - because the tax on buildings is immediately passed on to them in the form of higher space-rent, but in the long run the LRT cannot be passed on to them because the tax can't possibly decrease the supply of land.

The popularly held view that in the long run the property tax on both land and buildings is passed on to tenants is simply false – but even if it were true, then most tenants, just not all, will eventually pay less with LRT because it happens that most apartment buildings save big if buildings are taxes less than land (reason: big buildings on moderately priced residential land). The result is that apartment-building owners would save in the short run and apartment tenants would save in the long run.

The case is more mixed concerning office buildings. The owners of big new office-buildings will generally enjoy lower property taxes, but the owners of older smaller office-buildings will likely get property-tax increases because the higher taxes on their land value could outweigh the lower taxes on the older smaller buildings. But localities are likely to prefer new office-buildings to older smaller ones.

But *all* businesses that rent office space will eventually get rent reductions, for the reasons already cited. Most businesses rent.

All farmers, low incomers, elderly, temporarily unemployed, etc., would get tax decreases with a building-to-land tax shift if the law granted them exemptions.

It isn't only the tax on buildings that should be reduced, but other taxes on production also. For instance, cities should reimburse residents in whole or in part for their federal 6.2% social-security tax if land assessments were surtaxed; then every resident wage earner would get an immediate take-home pay increase and most residents would get a tax break.

Land tax good, all other taxes bad. Tax locations, not production.

Federal and State LRT

Now let us consider federal and state LRT. The federal government could substitute LRT for some of its onerous taxes on wages & capital. The appendix contains at least fourteen specific ways to implement a federal LRT.

There is ample precedent for a federal LRT. The federal government taxed land values (as part of real estate) in 1798, 1813, 1815, and 1861 under the never-repealed terms of Article 1, Section

2 of the Constitution, and the Sixteenth Amendment provides that Congress can tax income "from whatever source derived." The annual rent of land, whether imputed or actual, clearly qualifies as such income.

If the building owner and landowner are one and the same, the land rent income is imputed (assumed) - the building owners don't bother to transfer land rent from their building owner's pocket to their landowner's pocket (both pockets being in the same pair of pants). The localities and states tax the resultant land assessments and so can the federal government.

Congress has often taxed imputed income, as when it taxes waiters on their imputed income from tips. It also taxes the imputed income from zero-coupon bonds earned (but not collected) prior to maturity, also such corporate perks as free cafeteria meals and special parking privileges. If you should loan money to yourself, Congress will tax the imputed interest income of such a loan at an assumed rate known as the federal AFR.

Some people think that the LRT can never legally be anything more than a purely local or state matter, but they never cite any constitutional provisions for such a view, nor can they.

If a federal LRT replaces the regressive federal payroll tax, not only will *all* wage earners get a take-home pay increase, but also most voters will get tax reductions (since their wages are likely to be more than 100/6.2 (about 16.1) of their actual or imputed land rent income). See the appendix. If politicians can't win elections promising tax reductions to most voters, they're not going to win at all.

Many consumers are poor and are therefore especially hurt by taxes on things produced because such taxes raise prices; they run counter to the government's social-welfare expenditures. Subsidizing poverty is not a good way to eradicate it.

One last matter: some people think that LRT would promote anti-open-space growth. Not so, just the reverse; they should read chapter four. Workers and investors needn't be made to suffer to benefit the environment. Anyway, zoning can always be used to preserve open space.

How Will Land Prices Be Affected?

The direct effect of a constant increase in LRT is to cause land prices to sink to zero, for if the income from land is taxed away, there'll be no net income to the landowner, thus no land price. There'll be no income to sell. But with LRT, more will be produced on the land, especially if taxes on produced things are replaced, in which case land will become more valuable (and so will the LRT).

However, if the tax rate on land is steadily increased, approaching the relevant interest rate, then the annual land rent will eclipse the land price (we're not used to that), causing neophytes to think that as we approach 100% LRT and the price of land starts to disappear, land assessments might become too small to be assessed properly. Also, wouldn't we then be taxing more and more of less and less until we are heavily taxing nothing at all?

Don't worry about that. This conundrum can easily be avoided:

(1) We can leave a little land price un-taxed in order to have something to assess

(2) Or better, we could eventually switch to assessing only on the potential annual land-rent, rather than on land sale-price. Other countries assess this way.

Remember, for political reasons we should bring in the land value tax *gradually,* not all at once, to allow time for the minority of landowners to adjust to the new tax system.

Some might ask, "Why would people want to own land if they couldn't sell it eventually for a profit?" Answer: they could make a profit from its use because they wouldn't have taxes to pay on their labor and investments and the land would be cheaper to buy.

Technical: the sale price of land is equal to its annual after-tax net income divided by the relevant interest rate. Thus, if the net annual rent of a parcel of land after taxes is $3,000 and the expected return on land investments is 10%, that parcel's selling price would be $30,000 (i.e., $3,000 divided by .10). With full LRT, the sale price of land would eventually disappear (all the rent would be taxed away, so the sale price would be zero).

Natural-Resource LRT

Natural-resource land (containing oil, gas, metals, sand, etc.) may have to be taxed differently:

(a) The site should be leased at a moderate fixed yearly rental, thereby making it more likely that drillers will actually use the site.

(b) In addition, the natural-resource extractor should pay a certain percentage of the extracted natural resource in taxation (extractors usually prefer this way to be land-rent taxed); this is called a royalty. It may resemble a sales or severance tax, but it's not actually because the natural-resource extractor pays it for the use of land and thus it is land rent.

Similarly, when storeowners rent space in a shopping mall, they generally pay a percentage of their cash-register sales as rent in addition to their space rent. Both payments constitute their total space-rent.

The state of Alaska collects land-rent on its oil lands. According to the *U.S. News & World Report* (4/14/03, p. 42), the state has received $55 billion in oil revenues since the extraction of oil began about 1981. The state "each year pays a dividend of 20 percent of the state's oil profits to every citizen - $1,540 per person in 2002" (*Ibid.*). A family of four's share is likely to be four times that, or $6,160.

In addition, the Alaskan state government collects enough oil-land tax revenue so that it is one of the few U.S. states without any income or sales taxes – even though it isn't collecting the full LRT.

Imagine what Iraq or other oil-producing countries could distribute to their citizens if it had a 100% LRT (a dockworker's pay there is $30 a month).

Is LRT Liberal or Conservative?

Our contemporaries often insist on categorizing all new proposals as conservative or liberal, so let's not ignore this matter. Well, LRT is – both. It is conservative in that it down-taxes human production, a cardinal theme of conservatism. It is liberal in that it benefits the poor and creates job opportunities for them; it could also fund the government's anti-poverty efforts.

9

Steven B. Cord

Conservatives must realize that taxes on production have been rising steadily in every decade; occasional small tax cuts have only temporarily stemmed the rising tide of taxes. Increasing Social Security and Medicare expenses will ensure their continued rise in the future. The voters have become willing to pay taxes in order to get government services. In the long run, only LRT can save Republican Party principles.

Taxes and debt come to 30% in 1999 in America, 45% in France, Germany, Netherlands, and the U.K. (OECD, per IBD 3/30/04, A16). When we share in the benefits arising from the taxing of human production, that's tax socialism, and without LRT it's likely to get larger. Down-taxing labor & capital is a worthy goal, but it's only part of what is required and it won't happen extensively unless land is taxed.

With liberals the story is somewhat different. Liberals have been the principal LRT supporters so far. They tend to be open to new ideas and not so viscerally anti-every-tax, both the good and the bad. But they must realize that only LRT can effectively fund real anti-poverty efforts without taxing poor consumers. Taxing the rich is unsatisfactory – there's little revenue to be gained that way, and besides they provide more jobs than the average person.

Liberals must realize that while land-taxing raises revenue for the government, it helps the economy by ensuring that all land sites are used to their fullest potential (within zoning).

In the long run, LRT is the only way to permanently reduce taxes on production, which both conservatives and liberals could like. Maybe LRT could bring liberals and conservatives together. Both groups must realize that our economy will sputter and fail if production is heavily taxed and land rent is not.

It may be difficult to appeal simultaneously to both liberals and conservatives, but let us hope that ethical principles and hard empirical facts will guide them. Without LRT, they both will continue aiming at the wrong target. At least let us, dear reader, pledge to pursue the truth, which is not on the right or left, but beyond.

You can boil a frog in a frying pan, if you must, if you do it gradually enough; they're not smart enough to jump away. We can similarly tax labor & capital: if increased gradually enough,

10

they will continue producing, but free enterprise will eventually disappear, creating a need for still more taxation of labor & capital. We'll hardly realize we're taxing ourselves into socialism. For more on LRT, the reader is urged to visit www.EconomicBoom.info.

14 Differences

LRT Is different than all other taxes in every respect - but one. The exception: like all taxes, LRT raises revenue for the government. There the similarity ends. Abruptly. The many differences between LRT and all the other taxes arise because land is not produced by human labor whereas everything else of value is. Let's get specific:

1. *Property Rights Protected* – If land values are not taxed, then labor & capital must be, thereby violating property rights. Others partake of your labor when what you produce is taxed. That you share in their property via the taxation of their labor & capital is socialism, but it's not justice. However, if a democratic government utilizes LRT, everyone would then have the equivalent of equal access to nature and there'd be no need to invade private property rights via taxation.

The taxation of labor & capital is robbery, plain and simple - see chapter two for a fuller explanation. In fact, in a later chapter we'll see how a Citizen's Dividend is possible – the government could be paying taxes to us!

2. *Labor Benefits* – When we tax produced things, we tax the labor that made them, but no one made land so a tax on land is not a tax on labor. If labor isn't taxed, workers will bring home more money.

3. *Production Goes Up* – Taxes on produced things reduce production, but when we tax land values, we promote production because land-sites will have to be productively used (inadequate land uses will be uneconomic).

Many economic benefits were ascribed to the minuscule tax cut of 2003, but imagine the economic boom that would result from the substantial tax cut LRT would make possible!

4. *Prices Go Down* – Tax labor and capital and we increase prices; for example, a 5% sales tax on a dollar pen requires it to be

sold for $1.05. But land prices will fall if they're taxed. Lower land prices benefit poorer producers in particular because they borrow at higher interest rates; with LRT, they needn't. A zero land price will indicate that all the annual land rent is being collected in taxes.

Should land values be taxed at more than the annual rent of land? No, because then we would be taxing wages and investments. There's only so much land rent in an economy at any given moment; don't try to get blood out of a turnip.

5. *Passing on the tax* – All taxes are passed on to consumers and raise prices - except the land tax. Reason: when human-produced goods and services are taxed, their prices will have to be raised to pay the tax; at the higher price, less will be bought, and therefore produced, and so the higher price will stick.

But a tax on land values cannot possibly reduce the supply of land and so its price cannot be increased or passed on. It's a direct tax - the landowner must pay it, not the users. That's important because more than 30% of U.S. families rent (more in other countries) and most businesses rent. They don't own land so they won't be taxed.

6. *Builders will benefit from LRT* because it lowers land prices and un-taxes what they produce (buildings). Also, "holdouting" becomes unprofitable.

7. *Less unemployment* - When jobs are taxed (or when what they produce is taxed) jobs are lost, but not with LRT. If land is taxed more there won't be any less land; it will just be used more efficiently, thereby providing much-needed jobs.

8. *Less expensive assessment* – Assessing only land is obviously cheaper and more accurate than assessing both land and buildings.

9. *The efficient use of all land-sites* – with LRT, all land-sites would be put to their highest-and-best use (within zoning limits, of course), but all other taxes discourage the highest-and-best use of land.

10. *Ease of collection* – The income tax requires literally thousands of pages of nearly incomprehensible prose requiring hordes of lawyers and accountants and creating a vast underground economy. But land cannot be hidden; taxing it is relatively easy. LRT might require about three pages of explanation.

11. *The poor in particular would gain from LRT.* They collect little land rent and so would pay little LRT. In addition, they would

have greater access to land if land prices were lower. The things they buy will be cheaper (since those things wouldn't be taxed) and if jobs aren't taxed, there'll be less unemployment.

12. *Exports would boom.* We object (rightfully so) when foreigners put tariffs (taxes) on U.S. exports, but we do that to ourselves when we tax what gets exported. We make our own exports more expensive and therefore less competitive.

The U.S. leads all nations in taxing corporate profits as a percent of income (per OECD). That reduces U.S. exports, but LRT wouldn't require that.

13. *If you tax land, you tax it into use.* Tax anything else (like capital) and you tax it out of use.

14. *Single Tax.* When labor & capital are taxed, production is discouraged and GDP decreases, but the LRT actually increases the GDP; this increase actually increases LRT even more and enables it to become a Single Tax (but more on that later).

In short, whatever can be said about all other taxes, the exact reverse is true of LRT (except for raising revenue). Don't tax what's been produced; tax land rent instead. Tax the value of locations, not produced things.

(But LRT doesn't cure ingrown toenails, at least not directly.)

Some land value taxers have been so taken with these differences that they don't call the land value tax a tax. They have their reasons for re-defining the word "tax" but when they do so, they're not readily understood by their audience who use a different definition of the word.

Ability-to-Pay Considered

Ability-to-pay is a terrible principle of taxation – it's like the highwayman who says to his victim, "Stand and deliver! Your money or your life!" But since many people think highly of it, let's see how LRT would conform to it.

As it happens, LRT is the most ability-to-pay tax there is, even more than the income tax. Most people own little or no land rent so they would pay little LRT. For instance, is the potential income from the land you own a significant portion of your total income? Probably not. Poor people in particular don't own much taxable land – if they did they wouldn't be poor. But most everyone has an income.

Some luxury taxes might be more of an ability-to-pay tax than LRT, but they collect little revenue and only the envious could love them. Also, they are ethically deficient.

Some years ago a federal sales tax was levied on yachts ("only rich guys can own a yacht"). The consequences were disastrous - many yacht companies faced bankruptcy and blue-collar yacht employees lost their jobs. The tax raised little revenue, was unpopular and soon repealed.

The income tax is somewhat of an ability-to-pay tax, but LRT is much more so, because although almost everyone has an income, few people have a significant land-rent income. Anyway, the income tax is no longer the federal government's chief tax and the other federal taxes do not accord with ability-to-pay.

All tenants pay an income tax but as tenants they don't pay an LRT in the long run.

In 1978 a study by Anthony Pileggi, then a student at Indiana University of Pennsylvania but now a lawyer in Columbia, Md., found that 1.5% of the biggest landowners in Indiana, Pa., a town of about 15,000 population, paid 53.5% of the property tax on land values, but in that year the top 3% of income earners in the U.S. paid 30.6% of the federal income tax.

But Pileggi couldn't know all the interlocking landownerships in Indiana, as when people own land under family or corporate names; thus, the concentration of landownership in Indiana was even greater than his figures showed.

In towns larger than Indiana, LRT would be even more of an ability-to-pay tax because the ownership of land value is more concentrated and a greater percentage of residents are renters.

There are a number of studies concluding that a building-to-land tax shift is based on ability-to-pay. For instance, President Lyndon Johnson's Commission on Urban Housing found that "the share of land in housing values tends to rise with value of house and lot together" (p. 351).

If assessment exemptions, property tax exemptions, discounts, rebates, deferrals, circuit-breakers, caps, etc., were granted to the poor, elderly and temporarily unemployed, then LRT would be even more in accord with ability-to-pay. The appendix lists more such alleviations.

Wouldn't candidates for federal office (state and local, too) win elections if they advocated LRT? Maybe readers of this book will make LRT known to them.

The Greatest Secular Idea Ever Thought Of *Since The Beginning of Time*

Whoa! Isn't that a Big Claim? How could it be substantiated? Well, if what has been said already is true, it is justified, and wait till we get to the ethical considerations and wait till you see what has happened when LRT has actually been tried. Have patience. But you can be optimistic.

These are the changes you could expect from 100% LRT:
(1) No taxes on production
(2) Zero cost to buy land
(3) Untaxed development of all land-sites (within zoning limits)
(4) Lower prices for consumers
(5 More jobs, higher take-home pay
(6) All tenants would pay less space-rent eventually
(7) Less suicidal terrorism if production in underdeveloped economies could be down-taxed and land up-taxed. Terrorists and their supporters would then have this-world opportunities available to them.

It sounds almost too good to be true. But withhold final judgment.

If all these seven changes are true, then the claim is justified that LRT is the greatest secular idea ever thought of. If you encounter doubters, make sure they present logic and hard evidence for their point of view.

Maybe the unemployed should commit a crime and go to jail where they'll get three meals a day, free medical and dental benefits, and lots of time watching TV and building up their muscles. Most likely they'd get free college classes – all at no cost (to them). Many inmates are already doing that.

Some day, people will wonder why we were willing to tax production, not location. Probably it's because many people expect to suffer from taxation (it's possible to get used to sitting on a tack, or tacks). Isn't LRT the only way to prevent consigning free enterprise and democracy to the dustbin of history?

LRT is not alone in proving to be a hard sell. For instance, the privatization of social security could enable every worker to retire at least as a near-millionaire (just add up your expected income throughout your lifetime and then add 6.2% interest on them) yet it is still regarded as the third-rail of politics.

Don't under-estimate the power of irrationalism and habit.

To be sure, problems for LRT could arise in the future – such as the siren call that "we need a road, building, stadium, handout, etc., so let's tax production a little bit - that can't hurt much." Such siren calls should be opposed vigorously. Don't tax-rob your neighbor – or yourself.

On the other hand, once the movement toward LRT gains momentum, there may arise the urge to move faster toward 100% LRT than the voters are accustomed to accept, in which case retrogression might set in. We ought not disregard public opinion.

Our connection to Nature cannot be unimportant. Don't come to a final conclusion on this "Greatest Secular Idea" claim until you've seen its entire ethical justification and empirical support.

At the close of the Constitutional Convention in 1787, a woman asked Benjamin Franklin, "Well, Doctor, what have we got? A republic or a monarchy?"

"A republic," replied Franklin. "if you can keep it." (But the alternative to a republic these days is not a monarchy but a dictatorship with the trappings of a democracy, the transition being so gradual as to be almost unnoticed.)

> *Ralph Waldo Emerson, in 1859, is reputed to have said in despair about America, "No man living will see the end of slavery."*

2

We can rightfully own what we produce with our own labor, but since no one produced land, no one can rightfully own it unless a tax equal to its worth is paid to everyone else; then we won't be violating private property rights via taxation and everyone will have equal access to natural opportunities.

Landowners (as landowners) produce nothing (certainly not the land) and ought not claim what labor & capital have produced.

Shouldn't we all have equal access to natural opportunities or to what God has made for all of us equally to share? That's only possible if this book's proposal is enacted.

The chapter is followed by an interesting and unusual page-long narrative poem.

Chapter **2**

Ethics Requires It

I enter hesitatingly upon this chapter because many people consider ethics to be a matter determined by religion, but this book does not question or discuss religion at all; it only intends to find a rational basis for ethical beliefs and apply it to land taxation. Rationalism can and should *aid* religion (religion goes beyond the rational but it certainly embraces the rational). There's should be no conflict between the two).

Let us seek the ethical truth together. If ethically we should tax land values, then let's start doing it. If it's ethical, we can presume it will work well economically. So let's proceed carefully.

We can start with the generally accepted proposition that *we each own ourselves.* That seems obvious enough; the alternative is slavery. The slaveowner legally owns someone else, and we all know that's ethically wrong.

If we each own ourselves, then we each own our own labor. It is the product of our brain, nerves and muscles. Thus, we own what

19

we put our labor into, which then becomes our property. *Labor is the sole justification for private property.* If you freely buy someone else's labor, you have bought a just title.

A brief word about such intermediaries as truckers and retailers: they bought a just title to those goods or services from those who labored to produce them. We can presume they didn't steal the goods or services they're selling; they're innocent until proven guilty. The final consumers can morally buy these just titles.

But no one can justifiably own land - or fresh air, sunlight, the wind, oceans, the moon, planets, or stars - since no one made them. God got there first; He gave the earth to all of us equally; He didn't play favorites. Or if you prefer, we should all have equal access to nature. The first settlers may have put their labor into a crop or building on land but neither they nor anyone else made the land. No one can make location.

In fact, land is not distributed equally. For instance, in Colombia, 3% of the population owns 60% of the arable land. In Venezuela, 1.7% owns 74.5%. In Chile, 2.2% owns 75% (from John Gunther's *Inside South America,* 1967). In America, 3% of the population owns 95% of the land (USDA study, 1978).

But practicality demands private ownership of land, so what to do? Practicality seems to contradict ethical principle.

Fortunately, there's an elegant way out of this conundrum: let people own land privately so they can develop it as they wish (without tax penalty, be it noted) but let the government, representing all of us, collect the annual land rent through taxation. The government can then provide services equally to all. In other words, *land ownership should remain private but let landrentownership be public.* There would then be no taxation of labor & capital to violate private property rights.

I shouldn't share what you produce, but I do if I enjoy the government services funded by the taxes on your labor. You pay, I enjoy: not right. You do likewise to me – still not right. I rob you, you rob me - that's no way on which to base a society.

Then there's something else: LRT would motivate landowners to use their land-sites efficiently, for if they didn't, they'd have too much tax expense covered by a paltry income from an inadequate improvement. With no taxes on jobs or on goods and services, there would be a plethora of those good things; the plethora would further increase if all land-sites were used efficiently (within zoning limits).

Thus, LRT is a tax that actually creates jobs. This year, about $600 billion (undoubtedly more) in U.S. land rent is being misappropriated – no small matter; that's about $2000+ per capita per year (or $8,000+ yearly for a typical family of four). But political necessity absolutely demands that the tax be introduced gradually.

Labor & capital are entitled to divide up the entire GDP since they produced it. But a third party, the landowner, who as such produces nothing, arrives to demand a share of the GDP, which means that labor and capital don't get all they produced and are entitled to. Two produce, but three share. The law allowing that is unethical.

Poverty and unemployment are mainly the fruits of injustice. If land values were taxed, there needn't be any taxes on production. There needn't be any poverty, unemployment, or urban sprawl into the clean-and-green countryside. Just continuous prosperity for all.

All people should get the value of what they produce. But the rental value of land is produced by nature (to which we should all have *equal* access), or by society (which should protect our *equal* rights), or by government (over which we should all have *equal* control). Thus, the rental value of land belongs *equally* to us all, which can most practically be accomplished by taxation.

When the government builds a road, nearby land rents skyrocket. Shouldn't the government collect those land rents to pay for the road? Isn't the same true when the government provides any land-value-enhancing government service, such as schools, police and fire protection, social security, etc.?

It's very nice that you don't sneak into other people's homes at night and burgle -but if you benefit from the taxes they pay on their labor & capital, what's the difference? OK, they rob you likewise. That's socialism. But it isn't Justice.

Society shouldn't set each against the other, letting each steal what can be stolen and letting the devil take the hindmost – we can do better than that. God or Nature provides a natural governmental revenue.

> *Henry George:* "Suppose that instead of taking Friday as his slave, Robinson Crusoe had informed him that he was a free and independent citizen, entitled to vote and hold office, but that particular island was his (Robinson Crusoe's) private and exclusive property. What would have been the difference? Crusoe's ownership of the island would have been equivalent to his ownership of Friday."

Proving Equal Rights as the Rational Ethical Standard

At this juncture, an ethical skeptic is apt to exclaim, "Wait a moment! You assume that we each own ourselves, but assumptions aren't proof."

This is a legitimate contention. It certainly is invalid to base ethical reasoning on a conclusion, in this case "each person owns him or herself." Proof is required. Well, here it is:

(1) We have the right to be free to do what we should do - that's what "the right to be free" means, but what should we do?

(2) We should treat things as they are – that's being realistic and it is the essence of rationality.

So *we have the right to be free to treat things as they are.* But since we should always treat things as they are, we can assume it to be so, which leaves us with the right to be free, Q.E.D.

For example, if I have snow on my sidewalk, I should treat the snow as being there, and if I should clear it off my sidewalk, I obviously have the right to do so, which no one should interfere with.

Let us now proceed to prove the rights to life and property. Since we have the right to be free, then we must have the right to life – we couldn't have the right to be free otherwise. Our life is the sum total of all our freedoms.

Since we should own our labor, we should own what we put our labor into. The forced appropriation of our labor by others via taxation is therefore ethically wrong.

Mere purchase alone cannot justify ownership - of land or anything else. You can purchase a slave, stolen goods, or a share in a monopoly, but all you purchased was a defective ethical title. Only labor can ethically justify ownership. Only other people's labor should be freely purchased.

Since all our rights are more than any one of them, the right to life takes precedence over the right to be free. Similarly, the right to be free takes precedence over the right to our labor and property.

The taxation of labor & capital is a clear violation of the individual's right to property. It takes from those who labored (or bought the labor of others) and gives to those who didn't. The government should tax something that is not a product of human labor.

An important word here about means: they are part of their ends and are meant to accomplish those ends most effectively; if their ends are ethical and the means efficient, then those means are ethical. To be sure, we should be extremely wary of means that are intrinsically unethical.

Can the ends justify the means? Of course - that's what ends are for. The ultimate end is equal rights; all other apparent ends are really means to that ultimate end.

For instance, a killer comes to us, asking for the whereabouts of his intended victim. Surely we should lie - protecting a life is more important than lying.

Should we kill a person who steals our wallet? No, because the right to life takes precedence over the right to property; it includes more rights.

Surely, if you abhor murder, sex & race discrimination, and robbery, aren't you granting others their equal rights to life, liberty and property? You don't really believe in equal rights unless you actively support LRT.

All this is fully explained in an important and easy-to-read book, *Society at the Crossroads*. I can highly recommend it to the reader (full disclosure: I wrote it myself; write me to obtain a copy). It advocates LRT, but it does more than that. It tells why we have such pervasive social problems as crime, drug use, family and school collapse, violence in entertainment, etc. and what we can do about them. Its thesis leads logically to the war on terrorism.

The Four Ethical Justifications of LRT

Having established firm ethical principles, we are ready to consider the four ethical justifications for LRT:

Reason #1: *Equal rights demands LRT.* That we have equal rights needs no further elaboration. Let's see how it justifies LRT.

Labor is the sole justification for private property, but since no labor made land (location), its private ownership cannot be justified. The only practical solution is land rent taxation.

A private land<u>rent</u>owner partakes of the labor of others; a slaveowner does likewise. Both are equally wrong. Both are equally immoral.

All wealth is the result of the efforts of the active producers, labor & capital (the latter being the result of labor) who are entitled to all they've made. Because *all* produced wealth rightfully belongs to them, there is nothing left for landowners to justifiably claim - if they get something, they are necessarily denying labor & capital the full fruits of their efforts.

Since private property in land is practical and necessary, we should let land be privately owned so long as its annual rent is collected by the government in taxation for the use of everyone equally. Then everyone can equally enjoy the benefits of private landownership and uninvaded private property rights.

To sum up Reason #1: labor is the sole justification of ownership, and since no one made land, no one can justifiably own its annual rental income.

Private property in land rent is a bold, bare, enormous wrong like that of chattel slavery.

Reason #2: *Equal rights depend on equal access to the opportunities provided by nature.* Such equal access requires equal land ownership or more practically the equal distribution of land rent via LRT.

It is often said that we all should have equal opportunity, but it is careless to say that - we don't want to give equal opportunity for both the burglar and his victim. What we really favor is equal opportunity limited by the equal rights of others. This requires equal access to the resources of nature (E.A.R.N.) which in turn requires either the equal distribution of land, or more practically, the equal distribution of land rent.

> *Henry George:* "*The equal right of all men to the use of land is as clear as their equal right to breathe the air.*"

Nature is the common heritage of all people that can only be practically accomplished these days *not* by the constant re-division of land equally among us all but by allowing private landownership coupled with land rent taxation. Only then could we dispense with the unjust (and uneconomic) taxation of labor & capital.

Earth right = birthright.

Reason #3: *The origin of all land titles is in force and fraud and hence invalid.* When we trace back legal land titles to their origin, we find they rest on conquest, not on ethics; on the sword, not on the pen. It wasn't so long ago that Americans bludgeoned Indian tribes and took their land, although since that time the passage of land titles has been primarily ethical.

But Indian tribes bludgeoned their predecessors, so their land titles weren't ethically valid either. Cry not for the Indians over the loss of their landownership. Their force and fraud was also invalid. However, they surely have equal rights to landownership (not more-than-equal rights) and should share equally in land rent taxation.

Land titles the world over are no better ethically; ultimately, they also rest on bludgeoning, not on ethics. But that wrong can be righted only through LRT.

Philosopher Herbert Spencer expressed this interestingly - see the appendix.

Reason #4: *For many Americans, the Bible is the one true arbiter of right and wrong.* Here's how the Bible begins: "In the beginning God created the heavens and the Earth." Then God gave the earth (land) to all humanity. Isn't it blasphemy to claim ownership of God's gift to all of us? He didn't give the earth to some of us more than to others.

Then we read in Exodus that before the conquest of Canaan, Joshua promised the God-chosen people that the Canaanite land would be divided up equally by lot (which may have been the origin of the word's use to denote a land-site).

To keep the land division roughly equal, Leviticus 25:10 commands: "And ye shall hallow the fiftieth year and proclaim liberty throughout all the land to the inhabitants thereof: it shall be a jubilee unto you: and *ye shall return every man unto his land,* and ye shall return every man unto his family" (italics added).

Leviticus thereby specifies that in the Jubilee year – every fiftieth year - each man (representing his family) shall regain ownership of his allotment of land, which had been given equally to every family but which may have been mortgaged in the fifty-year interim. This arrangement suited an agricultural pre-urban society, but today we have to apply the same principle differently.

Or perhaps you prefer Leviticus 25:23: "The land shall not be sold forever: for the land is Mine; ye are strangers and sojourners with Me." Today we can do this most practically not by equally dividing up the land as by having a Jubilee, but by equally dividing up the land's annual rental income instead.

If you don't believe that God made the world and therefore owns it, then you don't really believe in God. If He owns it and we are all equally His children, then the earth belongs to those who can best develop it with their own labor & capital. But the land-rent income belongs equally to us all. Only a democracy will collect the rent and give it to all of us equally in the form of money or benefits. Democracy can be justified in no other way.

Then there's Leviticus 27:30: "All tithes on land levied on the produce of the soil or on the fruit of the trees (i.e., land rent) belong to Yahweh," not to some people more than others.

Don't overlook Psalm 23:1 – "The world and all that is in it belongs to the Lord: the earth and all who live on it are His." In other words, the earth (land) is the Lord's, not yours or mine, and we should all share equally in the Lord's gift to us all (also, human beings belong to the Lord, not to humans).

The ethical principle behind all these Biblical precepts is clear: no person should own outright the income from land. No one should claim God's gift to all His children.

John L. Kelly of Peoria, in his book *Kingdom of God,* provides conclusive evidence that this Biblical attitude towards land ownership was practiced for centuries in ancient Israel, enforced by the Jubilee year. Jesus referred favorably to it, though the Gospel accounts do not so specify.

We have heard, "Our Father who art in Heaven, Thy will be done on earth as it is in heaven." Fine, but note that in heaven, the inhabitants do not own land.

The view that landownership differed from other types of ownership persisted into the Middle Ages. The king, who ruled by divine right and represented the government was regarded as the ultimate landowner. This attitude is to be found today in the phrase "re(g)al estate," and in the governmental right of eminent domain.

For an individual to appropriate what God gave equally to us all – that's blasphemy!

If we violate ethics, we suffer economically. There are real live people walking around jobless in our midst, fearing the morrow, enduring poverty and suffering. We can end all that by fully applying provable ethical principles.

To what extent is this pitiful state of affairs due to your inaction?

> *Thomas Jefferson:* *"Whenever there are in any country uncultivated lands and unemployed poor, it is clear that the laws of property have been so far extended as to violate natural right."*

Further Objections of the Ethical Skeptic

But at this juncture, an Ethical Skeptic might voice serious objections that we ought to consider:

Skeptic: "Landowners contribute land to the productive process, so aren't they entitled to a return every bit as much as capitalists and laborers?"

Answer: "No. Only the contribution of labor can justify ownership, and neither landowners nor slaveowners contribute labor to the productive process. But labor & capital do. Labor obviously contributes labor, and capitalists contribute a labor-produced commodity (capital), so their ownership is just and logical.

"Monopolists and thieves also contribute to the productive process - they buy and sell things and you can buy shares of what they have appropriated – but as monopolists and thieves they don't

27

contribute productive labor. It's not contribution but labor that justifies ownership."

Skeptic: "We're all equal in that we all are free to buy land."

Answer: "Yes, but only labor can justify ownership, not purchase. We can buy shares of a monopoly, but that doesn't justify monopoly. We can buy stolen goods, but they're still stolen. We can even buy slaves. Mere purchase alone can't justify ownership."

Skeptic: "Equal rights is fine talk, but what is really ethical is – what works.

Answer: "Yes, equal rights is fine talk, but it also happens to work (see the next chapter). Anyway, success is not the true measure of ethics; many criminals are successful."

Skeptic: "Shouldn't we distinguish between ethical principles and the moral applications of those principles?"

Answer: "Yes. Ethical principles are how rational people treat (act toward, deal with) reality, so those principles are provable, but the correct moral application of these principles to specific real problems is not so clear because we can't always ascertain all the relevant facts and relationships in reality."

Skeptic: "Isn't stock-market speculation as justified as land speculation?"

Answer: "No. Corporate stock is ethically ownable, being the product of labor; thus it can be ethically bought and sold. But profits from land speculation can never be justified because they are not based on labor."

Skeptic: "Don't the original settlers have a right to own the land they have discovered, and cannot they then pass down this right to their heirs?"

Answer: "No. The original settlers only found a portion of the earth that rightfully belonged to everyone equally, including the not-yet-born. It's not like they found a lost coin, the owner of which cannot be determined. We should know who the rightful landowners are: they are everyone who ever lived - past, present and future."

"Many of the original settlers were farmers - they put their labor *into* a crop; they never made any land. For practical reasons, let them *legally* bequeath the land, but *ethically* the rent of it belongs equally to us all. As we all recognize, the ethical law is the higher law to which we all appeal when we criticize the legal laws."

"What about the original landowners who were land speculators; what right of labor can they claim?"

> *Henry George:* "Some people say that all rights are derived from the state, but they do not really think this; for they are as ready as anyone else to say of any proposed state action that it is right or it is wrong, in which they assert some standard of action higher than the state."

Skeptic: "Why own land if its annual rental income is taxed away?"

Answer: "Own it to make money developing it. That development needn't be taxed."

Skeptic: "If the majority says private land*rent*ownership is ethical, then its ethical. I believe in majority rule."

Answer: "So do I, but the majority isn't always ethically correct. Majority rule shouldn't force us to share our rightful property with others via taxation, nor should it allow some of us to have greater access to nature than others. Majorities should always be limited by the equal rights of individuals.

Skeptic: "If labor is the sole justification of private property, then surely you oppose inheritance."

Answer: "Not at all. We shouldn't oppose gifts, even after-death gifts."

Skeptic: "I suppose if we all respect the equal rights of each other, then we'll all be happier because we won't have murder, sex/race discrimination, or robbery."

Answer: "Probably, but happiness isn't the proper standard of ethics. Some people are happy if they murder, discriminate as to sex & race, and rob, yet such actions are unethical. Some Mafia capos die happy; that doesn't mean they were ethical. Happiness isn't even measurable, but LRT is."

Skeptic: "Well, I still have the same opinion I started out with."

Answer: "If you say so: 'Those convinced against their will are of the same opinion still.'"

Uncivilized
by Edmund Vance Cooke

An ancient ape, once on a time
Disliked exceedingly to climb,
And so he picked him out a tree
And said: "Now this belongs to me.
I have a hunch that monks are mutts,
And I can make them gather nuts
And bring the bulk of them to me,
By claiming title to this tree."

He took a green leaf and a reed
And wrote himself a title-deed,
Proclaiming pompously and slow
"All monkeys by these presents know."
Next morning when the monkeys came
To gather nuts, he made his claim:
"All monkeys climbing on this tree
Must bring their gathered nuts to me,
Cracking the same on equal shares
The meats are mine, the shells are theirs."

"But by what right? They cried, amazed,
Thinking the ape was surely crazed.
"By this," he answered; "if you'll read
You'll find it is a title-deed,
Made in precise and formal shape
And sworn before a fellow ape
Exactly on the legal plan
Used by that wondrous creature, man
In London, Tokyo, New York,
Glengarry, Kalamazoo and Cork.
Unless my deed is recognized,
It proves you quite uncivilized."

But said one monkey, "you'll agree
It was not you who made this tree."
"Nor," said the ape, serene and bland,
Does any owner make his land.
Yet all of its hereditaments
Are his and figure in his rents."

The puzzled monkeys sat about;
They could not make the question out.
Plainly, by precedent and law,
The ape's procedure showed no flaw;
And yet no matter what he said
The stomach still denied the head.

Up spoke one sprightly monkey then:
"Monkeys are monkeys, men are men;
The ape should try his legal capers
On men who may respect his papers.
We don't know deeds; we do know nuts,
And spite of 'ifs' and 'ands' and 'buts'
We know who gathers and un-meats 'em,
By monkey practice also eats 'em.
So tell the ape and all his flunkeys,
No man-tricks can be played on monkeys."

Thus, apes still climb to get their food,
Since monkey's minds are crass and crude,
And monkeys, all so ill-advised,
Still eat their nuts, uncivilized.

(1919)

3

Presented here is the mountain of hard empirical evidence that has been promised. Brief summaries of 22 *empirical* studies of existing applications are given; fully 215 more such studies are available upon request.

These studies are based on government documents (building-permits issued). They all show that the proposal has *always* been followed by a spurt in construction and renovation.

My own 18 empirical studies (in Pittsburgh, Harrisburg, Scranton and elsewhere) completely confirm these findings; Pittsburgh's long experience with the proposal is particularly illuminating.

Would any reasonable person need more hard evidence?

These benefits came from partial applications of the land value tax. If it were fully applied, we could expect the benefits to be much greater.

The piddling tax reduction of 2003 has been hailed as a great economic booster, but imagine the economic boost if taxes were replaced altogether! Wouldn't poverty and unemployment then disappear?

Chapter **3**

The Evidence

It shouldn't be necessary to list the economic benefits of <u>land rent taxation (LRT)</u> since it has already been demonstrated to be ethical. If it's ethically right, we can be sure it will produce economic benefits. But let's examine the vast empirical (factual) record anyway.

To get *empirical* evidence for LRT in the U.S., I had to induce localities to shift some of their property tax from buildings to land; only then could I measure the effects of LRT. I therefore induced 20 localities (all cities except for a downtown business-improvement district and a school district) to adopt a two-rate building-to-land LRT. This necessitated about 45 additional rate expansions in these localities. This took me twenty years to do.

This enabled me to do seventeen empirical studies to see what impact the building-to-land tax switch had on new construction and renovation. One study – my eighteenth – tested the reverse: a land-to-building switch. Whenever possible, I compared the two-rate LRT cities with their one-rate but otherwise comparable neighbors who presumably were subject to the same economic-growth influences.

I was able to access *original* documents; they were building permits carefully kept on file at the various city halls (building permits have to be taken out for all construction and major renovation projects). In most cases, it was necessary to actually visit these city halls - no easy task. It required long car trips and overnight stays in sometimes not-so-good motels. Some jurisdictions could not or at least did not give me the information I needed.

This is what I found: new construction and renovation, as measured by building permits issued, was *always* greater in the three years after the building-to-land switch than in the three years before. What's more, in the one case where there was a reverse land-to-building switch, the expected huge decline in new construction and renovation ensued. Hard factual proof in 18 studies out of 18!

But it gets even better: the two-rate LRT localities *always* out-constructed and out-renovated their one-rate neighbors whenever building-permit comparisons could be made.

What's more, in all my reading (which has been fairly extensive on this subject) I never encountered any studies contradicting these findings.

H. Bronson Cowan of Canada and Allan Hutchinson of Victoria, Australia had done similar research, starting in 1943. They conceived the idea of examining the building permit records to see if a switch to land value taxation spurred new construction and renovation. This they could easily do because the Australian government listed permits for every municipality in the country in its annual statistical report. The necessary building-permit figures came to them, they didn't have to go to them.

They (particularly Hutchinson) began to compare the building permit issuance in the Australian cities that switched to LRT, both before and after the switch. In every case, they found that cities increased their new construction and renovation after they shifted their building tax to land.

Even better, they found that land-taxing cities always out-constructed and out-renovated neighboring non-land taxing cities that were presumably subject to the same economic influences. They did hundreds of such studies. My studies in America produced the same results.

While doing research for this book, I thought I'd include some empirical studies, so I reviewed the past issues of *Incentive Taxation,* a newsletter I have edited from 1974 to 2004.

I found a plethora of such studies, many more than I had expected. I stopped after listing 237 studies, thinking that few people would read that many - yet I had only reviewed about a quarter of the past issues and I have many more in my files! I could easily gather about a thousand such studies.

I'll send brief summaries of the 237 studies to anyone wanting them – at a cost of $12 by post, $4 by email, as of 2005. A representative 22 of these studies are presented here.

If all these *empirical* studies fail to convince people that LRT induces economic prosperity and tax reduction for most voters, then what will? What more could they legitimately require before they act, either as private citizens or as public officials? If a little LRT works well, should we not expect that 100% LRT would work even better?

Most people don't own much land-rent income, so that if such income is collected in taxes, they would get tax *reductions* without any reduction in government revenue.

That's especially true for poor people. For instance, two census-tract studies in 2002 done by the Center for the Study of Economics found that the biggest percentage declines occurred in poor neighborhoods. In addition, all poor tenants would benefit.

> *Why do most localities tax land and buildings - two entirely different entities - at the same rate? Why do American voters allow themselves to be unintentionally impoverished by state and federal taxing authorities?*

The EMPIRICAL Record

First of all, let's review briefly the 237 empirical studies. They present hard evidence that LRT has always worked in actual practice; as it happens, LRT has a fairly extensive record in the world, though not as a Single Tax and not much in America, so that it becomes possible to see what results LRT has had. We needn't theorize only. There is a rather extensive empirical record we could examine.

Here is a summary of these 237 studies:

➢ 45 studies conclude that when a town adopts land rent taxation, a spurt in new construction and renovation results.

➢ *63 studies conclude that towns switching from taxing buildings to taxing land always out-constructed and out-renovated their comparable neighbors who were subject to the same economic-growth influences.*

➢ 83 studies concluded that most voters paid less with a revenue-neutral building-to-land tax switch. In 2 studies, most voters paid slightly more. Of course, the government lost absolutely no revenue at all.

➢ 30 studies concluded that LRT had various miscellaneous advantages - for example, tax defaults decreased, which is what you would expect if buildings are taxed less.

➢ 6 studies concerned farmers: in three studies, farmers essentially broke even with a shift to LRT, in one study farmers would pay slightly more, and in two studies farmers would pay slightly less. Australian farmers have generally voted to adopt LRT.

➢ 8 studies listed endorsements (also, there are literally hundreds of endorsements by prominent authorities listed elsewhere).

The following are brief summaries of 22 of these 237 empirical studies:

(1) The contiguous cities of *Allentown* and *Bethlehem* in eastern Pennsylvania are comparable as to size and economy. In 1997 Allentown became two-rate LRT; its difference between land and building rates was expanded in that year and in each of the following four years while Bethlehem remained one-rate.

Allentown's new private construction and renovation grew by 32% in dollar value in the three years after it first adopted two-rate LRT as compared to the prior three years. That was

1.8 times more than Bethlehem's increase in private construction and renovation even though Bethlehem (but not Allentown, be it noted) was the recipient of much federal-grant money during 1997-99.

These figures are based on a study of city-hall building-permit data on file in the Allentown and Bethlehem city halls, done by Benjamin Howells (science researcher and former Allentown councilman), William Kells (science-oriented businessman) and Steven Cord (professor-emeritus) in 1999. The study was summarized in *Incentive Taxation* (IT, 7/00).

(2) *Washington* and nearby *Monessen* (both in southwestern Pennsylvania) are roughly comparable as to size and economy. After Washington shifted some of its tax off buildings onto land in 1985, its new private construction and renovation *increased* by 33% in dollar value in the three years after its two-rate adoption as compared to the prior three years. During the same time period, nearby one-rate Monessen's new private construction and renovation *decreased* by 26%.

A report of this study, based on building-permit data on file in the Washington and Monessen city halls, can be found in IT, 10/88, 10/97 and 9/00).

(3) *Connellsville, Pa.* saw its new private construction and renovation jump 3.46 times in the three years after it adopted a two-rate LRT property tax as compared to the prior three years. This jump can be compared to the rather modest 1.07 increase in nearby *Uniontown's* new private construction and renovation during the same time period. The two cities are quite comparable, although Uniontown is somewhat larger and is the county seat (both are economic-development plusses).

A report of this study can be found in IT, 10/97. It is based on building-permits issued and on file in the Connellsville and Uniontown city halls.

(4) *Aliquippa, Pa.*, went two-rate LRT in January 1988 after the closure of its large steel mill, whereupon its new private construction and renovation jumped 97% in the three years after the two-rate switch as compared to the three-years-before. See IT, 10/91.

Nearby *Ambridge,* comparable except that it was closer to the Pittsburgh international airport and enjoyed brisk tourist traffic at its Old Economy Shaker Village (both economic plusses), experienced a 30% decline in private building-permits issued during the same periods of time. Nearby *Beaver Falls,* also comparable except that it is less hilly than Aliquippa and is the county seat (again, economic plusses) experienced a comparable 7.2% decline during the same period of time.

In July 1993, the *Aliquippa School District* adopted a two-rate building-to-land switch in its property tax. Its new private construction and renovation thereupon spurted: for 1994-95, it was 2.3 times greater than for 1991-92 (based on building-permit records on file at city hall; see IT, 12/99).

(5) In 1989, *Clairton, Pa.,* an industrial suburb of Pittsburgh, was under direct state fiscal control, officially labeled "financially distressed." It took the advice of the prestigious Pennsylvania Economy League and went two-rate LRT, taxing building assessments at 2.105% and land assessments at 10% (instead of both at 3.7%). During the three-year period after the switch, its taxable building permits were 8.5% more than in the three years before (based on building-permit records in Clairton City Hall). This is to be compared to the 5.8% decline in U.S. building permits during the same periods of time (see IT 10/93).

(6) *Oil City, Pa.* adopted two-rate LRT starting in January 1989 and increased its new private construction and renovation 58.2% in the three following years as compared to the three-years-before, while its nearby one-rate but otherwise comparable neighbor, Franklin, Pa., declined 12.2% in the same time periods (based on a study of building-permits issued in the two city halls; see IT 11/94).

(7) *Pittsburgh's* long two-rate LVT experience has provided many studies:

In the years 1980-84, when Pittsburgh was expanding the difference between its land and building property-tax rates, its new construction as measured by building-permits issued was fully 3.57 times higher, adjusted for inflation, than in the pre-change years of 1974-78, despite the steady post-1980 contraction of Pittsburgh's steel industry (source: Pennsylvania Economy League study of Pittsburgh's two-rate tax 1985, p. 16).

For the entire United States, 1980-84 office-building permits were only 1.6 times higher than for 1974-78 (not adjusted for inflation, per Daniel Sansbury, U.S. Bureau of Census, Suitland, Md., 1/21/93, see IT, 10/93).

The boom in Pittsburgh continued: in 1985, its building permits increased 2.29 times over 1984; in 1986, it was 2.38 times greater than in 1984 (source: Pbg. Bldg. Inspection Dept., see IT 10/86).

After Pittsburgh increased its land-tax rate (but not its building tax rate) in 1979 and again in 1980, its construction increased fully 6.2 times faster than U.S. construction during the same period of time (sources: table 1194, U.S. Census report C30, and the building-permit annual reports, city of Pittsburgh).

(8) Godfrey Dunkley, an economist and mechanical engineer specializing in the design and sale of fluid filtration equipment, extracted interesting statistics from the official Municipal Yearbooks of the government of *South Africa*.

He compared 1959 assessments to 1979 assessments and found that the one-rate towns (taxing land and buildings the same) increased their total assessments by 486%, but the two-rate towns (taxing land more than buildings) experienced a 561% increase and the 46 towns that taxed only land assessments experienced an 850% increase. Inflation affected all these figures, but note that the more a town taxed land values, the faster it grew.

Further substantiation from the same study: the eight towns that switched from one-rate to two-rate increased their assessments by 748%, and the 15 towns that switched to land-taxing-only increased by 996% (see IT 9/83). A later Dunkley study of a different time comparison yielded similar figures.

In January 2005, Dunkley wrote me, "to the best of my recollection, government property did not appear in the valuation rolls at that time."

(9) Then there's the study by professors Wallace Oates and Robert Schwab, both of the University of Maryland. They reported that 15 large northeastern cities in the U.S. averaged a

decline of 15.5% in their annual value of building permits issued between 1960-1969 and 1980-1989, but two-rate LRT *Pittsburgh* recorded a 70.4% increase.

Columbus, Ohio was the only other city in the study recording an increase - a rather modest 3.6% – but it had annexed some fast-growing suburbs in the interim (see IT, 10/92).

(10) In 1995, Professor Nicolaus Tideman of Virginia Tech University and his then-graduate student, Florenz Plassmann (now a professor at the University of Binghamton), completed a highly technical study of land value taxation in Pennsylvania entitled "A Markov Chain Monte Carlo Analysis of the Effect of Two-Rate Property Taxes on Construction." See IT 12/00 for the verbatim conclusion of the original study, and *Journal of Urban Economics*, 3/00, pp. 216-47, for the full study.

To quote from their conclusion:

"The results say that for all four categories of construction, an increase in the effective tax differential is associated with an increase in the average value per permit. In the case of residential housing, a 1% increase in the effective tax differential is associated with a 12% increase in the average value per unit... From the perspective of economic theory, it is not at all surprising that when taxes are taken off of buildings, people build more valuable buildings. But it is nice to see the numbers."

Although this study appeared in a peer-reviewed scholarly journal, it occasioned no citations in other scholarly journals or comments from other professional economists. It was like a stone dropped in a pond with no ripples.

(11) Harry Gunnison Brown, a prominent economist, reported that suburbs of *Melbourne*, Victoria, Australia, which were about five rail miles from Flinders Street in the center of Melbourne and which taxed land values only, had 50% more dwellings constructed per available acre in the 1928-1942 period than similarly situated suburbs which taxed land and buildings at the same rate (source: Aus. govt. statistics in "Public Charges Upon Land Values," a 1961 study prepared by the General Council of Rating [local taxing] Reform).

Making a similar comparison for suburbs seven miles out, the land-value-tax suburbs did 2.33 times better; LRT suburbs 9.5 miles out did twice as well.

(12) A *Pittsburgh City Council study* (1976) concluded that a 1% earned income tax would hit the city's homeowners 3.59 times harder than an equivalent-in-revenue LRT increase. The same study also found that a two-rate LRT would down-tax 73.6% of homeowners.

(13) A *Washington, D.C.* council-authorized study done in the 1970s concluded that if the current property tax were shifted from land and building assessments to land assessments only, there would be these tax reductions: single-family homes 18.1%, two-family homes 20.9%, row houses 14%, walkup apartments 8.9%, elevator apartments 22.5%.

(14) In 64 suburbs *outside central Melbourne* (Aus.) during the two-year period 1955/56 to 1957/58, there were 42 new factories, of which half were in the 17 localities using LRT-only. In addition, factory employment in these 17 LRT-only localities increased by 445 whereas in the remaining 47 localities, factory employment decreased by 361 (source: see #11 above).

(15) *Twelve studies in rural Victoria* found that the LRT-only towns averaged a construction-and-renovation growth of 29% as compared to the growth of their real-estate-income-taxing neighbors of a modest 2.6% in the same period of time (source: GCRR study of building-permits issued as reported in *Progress* Magazine, Melbourne 3/75). LRT-only was always adopted as a result of a poll of landowners only.

(16) If eastern Americans fall through the earth, they will emerge near *Perth, Western Australia* (pop. 400,000). 17 localities in that vicinity taxed land values only; they experienced a 34.36% *increase* in the total number of dwellings between 6/30/71 and 6/30/76. The nine nearby localities taxing both land and buildings and presumably subject to the same economic-growth influences experienced a 0.02% *decrease* in the same time period (source: Aus. govt. statistics, as cited in *Progress*, 11/77, p. 10).

(17) In *North Dakota*, according to USN&WR, 4/3/78, p. 54, farmers paid no tax on farm buildings. A survey by a high official of the N.D. League of Cities revealed that this has encouraged new farm construction.

(18) *California Irrigation Districts* - A 1909 California law required that when new irrigation networks were to be built, they were to be financed by a tax on the affected land values only; all privately owned improvements were to be property-tax exempt. The theory was that publicly owned irrigation networks increased land values so the expense of those networks should be borne by the affected landowners.

The result has been beneficial to the local farmers, particularly the smaller ones. The irrigated valleys are among the most productive in the world. This is what the Modesto Chamber of Commerce stated in 1914 (according to the Congressional Research Service in its study, "Property Taxation," p. 48):

"As a result of the change many of the large ranches have been cut up and sold in small tracts. The new owners are cultivating these farms intensively. The population of both country and city has greatly increased. The new system of taxation has brought great prosperity to our district. Farmers are now encouraged to improve their property. Industry and thrift are not punished by an increase in taxes."

(19) *Malvern, Australia* experienced a marked construction spurt after it adopted LRT-only in August 1955. The most extensive construction took place in its blighted problem neighborhoods. Before August 1955, those neighborhoods accounted for only 22% of the city's building permits, but in each of the five ensuing years that percentage jumped first to 35% and then steadily moved up to 47% in 1960 (these percentages are of continually larger construction figures; source - *Victoria Building & Construction Journal*, 1979).

(20) Tax defaults: in *New Zealand* in the late 1950s, ten large LRT-only cities had slightly less tax defaults than three large non-LRT cities, indicating that exempting buildings from local taxation does not increase tax defaults (see the 1961 report of the

Canadian Federation of Mayors and Municipalities, p. 31, by H. Bronson Cowan). See IT, 12/81.

(21) A city-funded 1980 study in *New Castle, Pa.* revealed that seven vacant and two poorly developed downtown sites would be an estimated $150,851 more profitable to build upon with an LRT-only property tax. If county and school taxes were also to adopt LRT-only, then the extra profit would be an estimated $243,750 a year.

(22) Random-sample studies in sixteen U.S. cities substantiated that most homeowners pay less with a two-rate building-to-land property-tax shift (IT 5-7/76).

It is possible to easily ascertain by exactly how much each voter in a city would fare with this two-rate approach *before* going public with the idea.

Many of these cases are from Australia – some people seem to think that Australians walk around upside down, but it isn't true. Anyway, there are many cases all over the world.

For more information about LRT, consult www.EconomicBoom. info. If you want the 237 empirical studies, let me know.

The Pittsburgh Study

But wait a moment – I just finished a study of Pittsburgh that I must tell you about. I can't restrain myself. This should be the Absolute Clincher. Wait till you read about this one.

The city of Pittsburgh was taxing land assessments more than building assessments ever since 1915, but since 2001 it reverted to taxing both types of assessments at the same one rate.

Why did it revert? An interesting question, but we can only consider it briefly here because it is essentially irrelevant to what we are investigating, which is "what effect did the land-to-building switch have?" Well, in 2000, the voters in Pittsburgh were aroused to fever pitch as never before by their property tax because their new land assessments were increased by five-to-eight times *overnight* - a political no-no.

The voters mistakenly thought that if the land tax rate were reduced to the lower building tax rate, their property taxes would be reduced (not realizing the building tax rate would have to be increased). They were unaware of the many LRT empirical studies that had been made. So they pressured their city council to equalize the property-tax rates on land and buildings. This is what happened:

Pittsburgh experienced a 19.57% <u>decline</u> in private new construction and renovation in the three years after rescission as compared to the three years before, even though during the same time period, the value of construction put in place nationwide (which included public construction) increased 7.7% and sales tax receipts in Pittsburgh increased 7.6%. Both of these increases should have boosted Pittsburgh's new construction, but they didn't.

It took me 200 hours of grueling labor to examine all 13,547 of the building permits for the six-year period. For the full details of the study, see *Incentive Taxation* (5/04).

Interestingly, a computer examination of the entire assessment roll of

Pittsburgh found that 54% of the homeowners paid *more* property tax with a land-to-building tax switch. What's more, *all* tenants will get an almost immediate space-rent *increase* from the newly increased building tax because it will be passed on to them in the form of higher space rents (but not so in the long run from an LRT increase – check any basic economics textbook).

These Pittsburghers acted somewhat like Samson. They brought the house down upon themselves.

This LRT rescission has actually been a blessing in disguise because it allows us to examine the effect of a land-to-building tax switch on construction and renovation.

The Significance of These Studies

Much more evidence for LRT could be cited, but I stop here because I don't want to tax your patience, dear reader. But it's common sense to expect that if you tax buildings less, you'll have more and better buildings. If you up-tax land, land-sites will have to be more efficiently utilized. You'll also get beneficial results from the un-taxing of any human-produced commodity or service. Don't let preconceived notions trump logic and hard empirical evidence. Don't deny reality.

It would seem reasonable to assume that if a moderate building-to-land tax shift produces great benefits, a 100% shift would provide even greater benefits.

Aren't 237+ empirical studies actually an embarrassment of riches, an overload, a plethora of facts, a reality storm, an empirical blizzard, a typhoon of hard evidence, and a veritable tsunami of observations based on original sources that we ignore only at the peril of widespread poverty and the constant threat of unemployment? To ignore these studies is to sink our society.

In some other empirical research I'm doing, I thought my evidence had contradicted the indisputable Law of Averages. Well then, my empirical research must be inadequate. But in this case, the empirical research is supporting something that is completely logical – namely, that when you down-tax produced things, you have more of them, and if you up-tax land values, then the land must be more productively used.

There is much more hard empirical evidence for LRT, but we needn't gild the lily. *Can we not now conclude that LRT is a tax that actually creates jobs and wealth?* Wouldn't it inundate poverty and unemployment (and the fear of them)? Shouldn't the whole world take cognizance of it? Imagine what LRT would accomplish in Iraq and Afghanistan. In the long run, is world peace possible without LRT?

Politicians instituting LRT must constantly inform voters of its benefits; they're not likely to be aware of them otherwise. Those benefits are not immediately apparent or might be ascribed to other things. Voters are accustomed to being tax-robbed and may wonder why this tax is beneficial and why the land tax rate should be so high. The need for education on this matter is constant.

The chief argument against LRT is that, yes, it's a good idea but it's not that important and isn't worth the effort to implement it. Well, the empirical evidence shows that it *is* important - even a slight tax-rate shift has produced noticeably good results. Imagine what a major tax-rate shift would have!

How Relevant is Regression Analysis?

Regression analysis is a technique for quantifying all the relevant factors in order to see what effect they might have. However, regression analysis in these 22 (or 237) cases could not possibly be value-free because the researcher must identify and quantify the relevant factors affecting construction in an urban environment – an impossible task.

This would involve many subjective value judgments. But if hundreds of *empirical* studies conclude that LRT has always worked well, and if the logical connection is perfectly clear, then we can feel confident that a cause-and-effect relationship has been proven.

I tried very hard to isolate factors other than building and land taxation that might affect the issuance of building permits; there were few, and as it happens I found more possible factors helping the one-rate cities than helping the two-rate cities.

Regression analysis would not have helped me at all. I have presented 22 empirical studies here and there are about a thousand such studies that could be cited. I did 18 of them myself. If I could cite only two studies, or maybe five, the empirical proof may not have been adequate, but 18, 22, 237, thousands? Let us have no truck with false objectivity.

Doubtlessly, regression analysis has a definite place in medical, biological, geological, etc. research. But the 22 studies listed here simply do not lend themselves to regression analysis.

If you encounter critics who doubt the economic benefits of LRT, **be sure to ask them to support their criticisms with hard cold** *facts* (but do it politely so as not to embarrass them unduly). Mere theoretical studies shouldn't count.

Don't ignore these empirical studies. Confront them head-on. Ask yourself, how else could we determine whether LRT works? Are you surprised that if you down-tax buildings or other human production, you'll have more of them and if land-sites are used more efficiently, then the production on those sites will increase? Isn't it reassuring that the logic is fully supported by the available facts?

Are you going to let little children starve and families live in poverty or one step above it – all because of unsupported preconceived notions? Are you going to let terrorism breed amidst grinding poverty? Now that you know how these evils can be eliminated, to do nothing is to evade responsibility.

The Broader Picture

The claim that LRT is necessary for the continuance of free enterprise and democracy must have sounded like an exaggeration when you first encountered it, but after confronting the impeccable logic and huge mass of empirical evidence supporting LRT (and much more could be presented), does it still sound like exaggeration? Isn't it likely that LRT could dispel involuntary poverty and unemployment if it were widely adopted? Couldn't 100% LRT provide continuous prosperity to us all?

Just imagine how wealth production would spurt if it were untaxed. If jobs were untaxed, unemployment (and the fear of it) would dwindle away. Employers would beg for workers. The poor in particular would be better off. So would we all.

If real social justice abounded, wouldn't crime decrease? Does it make sense to tax-penalize wealth production in order to subsidize poverty? *Isn't LRT a tax that creates jobs?*

Once you could reasonably regard pro-LRT claims as mere fulmination and exaggeration, but after you have seen the existing *empirical* evidence for LRT, can you do that now? And the ethical case for LRT – can you possibly ignore it?

How long can true democracy last if the government increasingly violates the private property rights of its citizens through taxation? Already these rights are being eroded in favor of mere majority rule.

Our world needs many reforms, but don't they all pale besides this one?

Taxes on labor and capital have been rising steadily in the past two centuries. Aren't they slowly extinguishing free enterprise and

47

democracy? If conservatives reject LRT, they must necessarily support the taxation of labor and capital; non-LRT liberals must do the same. We are likely to slowly slide into socialism.

As free enterprise fades away, it will be blamed for depressions and inflation. What replaces it won't be called socialism - probably compassion. And when democracy fades away, it will be replaced by "benevolent" dictatorship (but probably still called democracy). In the long run, an LRT-less free enterprise and democracy won't work and will be replaced.

Everywhere depressions have been countered with massive government deficits. Inflation is an ever-present spectre. We are essentially living off future generations – they'll pay the bills for the government goodies we now enjoy (that's a vast Ponzi scheme, isn't it?).

There'll come a time when the unrestrained inflation antidote to depression will simply not work because consumers and investors will anticipate rising prices and discount them; they won't be fooled for long into producing, but they'll lose their jobs. It was Keynes who said that in the long run we're all dead; meanwhile, we are supposed to eat, drink and be as merry as possible. But this particular long run may come sooner than he expected.

One easy way to make the LRT politically attractive is to replace the 7.65% payroll tax, in whole or in part, with a federal, state or local tax on land values. Then all wage earners would get take-home pay increases and most voters would get tax reductions. For more on this, see the appendix.

> *If you are influenced more by unsubstantiated preconceived notions than by fact (after fact after fact), what do you intend to get out of this book?*

"We honor Liberty in name and in form. We set up her statues and sound her praises. But we have not fully trusted her. And with our growth so grow her demands. She will have no half service!

"In our time, as in times before, creep on the insidious forces that, producing inequality, destroy Liberty. On the horizon the clouds begin to lower. Liberty calls to us again. We must follow her further; we must trust her fully. Either we must wholly accept her

or she will not stay. It is not enough that men should vote; it is not enough that they should be theoretically equal before the law. They must have liberty to avail themselves of the opportunities and means of life; they must stand on equal terms with reference to the bounty of nature. Either this, or Liberty withdraws her light!

"This is the universal law. This is the lesson of the centuries. Unless its foundation be laid in justice the social structure cannot stand."

It is altogether fitting that we end this chapter with the words of Henry George. It was he who first put forward the modern case for land rent taxation.

4

Land value taxation could help farmers and is absolutely necessary for environmentalism to really succeed. This may not be readily apparent so a careful explanation is necessary.

Concerning the war against terrorism: democracy is not likely to succeed in the Middle East unless it is accompanied by the prosperity induced by land rent taxation. Such a tax has particular application in the Middle East where land is oil-rich and wages are low.

A special Bonus concludes this chapter.

Chapter **4**

Pro-Farming, Pro-Environment, Anti-Terrorism
(and a Bonus)

From long experience, I know that whenever LRT is first proposed, the immediate response is, "You'll hurt farmers! You'll ruin the environment! Besides, what about terrorism?" So let's answer these concerns now.

LRT Is Pro-Farming

Before we get into the 8 ways by which LRT helps farmers, we must first know what modern farming is all about:

51

➢ Even though just about every farmer is genuinely concerned about the environment, we should realize that farming is the environment's #1 despoiler - through topsoil destruction and runoff, the use of polluting farm machinery, the use of dangerous chemicals, and the premature invasion of open space when agricultural land is used inefficiently.

Let us be concerned about farmers, but let us not romanticize farming. If the typical American ever saw a modern factory farm, with its penned animals bred for white meat and so misshapen they can't walk, and its computerized mechanized crop-tilling, they would soon lose their romantic visualization of the Farmer Brown image from the Dick & Jane books.

➢ No good defense of the farm subsidy program is possible. The subsidies go to the big farmers, not to the smaller needier ones. It does nothing for farm workers. It is unjust – it taxes some for the benefit of others. It is a big expense to the government. Farmland values jump because of the subsidies. Nevertheless, farm subsidies are used by governments the world over.

➢ Despite farm subsidies, the number of farmers has been dropping the world over, particularly in the United States where farmers are currently about 2.62% of the total workforce (*U.S. Statistical Abstract 1998*, table 675, citing U.S. Bureau of Labor Statistics, *Employment & Earnings* and unpublished data). The percentage keeps sinking, most of that 2.62% are hired hands (not landowners) and many farmers (most?) work off the farm.

Also, much farmland is rented, not farmed by the owner (in Ohio, for instance, 41% of the farmland is rented, according to the *Ohio Farmer,* 8/80). Effectively, the main farm landowners are banks, since most farmland is heavily mortgaged to them.

> ➤ If LRT were adopted only in urban localities where there are no farmers, they wouldn't be affected at all. To date, LRT adoptions in the U.S. have occurred only in urban localities.
> ➤ If LRT were adopted in purely farming localities, some farmers would pay more while other farmers would pay less, but as a group, farmers would pay exactly the same as before LRT.
> ➤ Farmers generally have higher incomes than non-farmers. *Forbes* magazine (5/17/99, p. 60) reported that "full-time farmers ages 35 to 44 averaged $61,344 net cash return last year, well above the overall average of $40,280." A USDA study in 1997 found that farm household income averaged $52,347 (which includes pay from off-farm jobs) compared with $49,692 for the average U.S. household.
> ➤ Farmers generally have more assets than non-farmers. "The average full-time farmer is 10 times wealthier than the average householder, with roughly $700,000 in assets. Farmers receive almost 45 cents in federal support for every dollar earned. The 30,000 largest operators receive, on an average, over $50,000 per year. And only $1 out of every $10 goes to needy farmers." (Richard Dennis in *Reason Magazine,* 4/93, p. 29). Why should poorer taxpayers subsidize those who richer?
> ➤ In Australia, New Zealand, South Africa, and Denmark, farmers have led the movement to spread LRT. Farmers can readily see that a farmer owning a fertile piece of land should earn no more than a neighboring farmer who works just as diligently but is less well situated. Fertility is a gift of God or Nature, not man-made (when fertility is enhanced by human effort, such effort should not be taxed).

Let us now see how LRT would benefit farmers:

(1) Farmers might own much land area, but the value of a farming acre is generally minuscule compared to an urban acre; since the LRT is on value, not acreage, we could expect farmers to pay less taxes

with LRT than with other taxes. There are more studies showing that farmers actually save with LRT than otherwise, though that may be because of agricultural use assessment (instead of market assessment).

If critics think that farmers would be more heavily taxed by LRT, they should present empirical studies proving that contention. Anyway, farmers can always receive special tax abatements. Then they surely wouldn't pay more.

(2) LRT would obviously result in the down-taxing of farm buildings and farm production.

(3) Our cities would become more developed with LRT, thereby containing the urban sprawl about which farmers justly and bitterly complain. If we green our cities, we'll blacktop our farms. By causing the efficient use of land, LRT would prevent premature land development.

(4) LRT would cause rural land to be used more efficiently, leading to less development pressure on land that should remain undeveloped (such land has little market value, so it would have little LRT).

(5) 100% LRT would reduce farmland prices, thereby benefiting new young farmers looking to enter farming. They wouldn't be burdened with huge land mortgages before they begin to farm. Without LRT, we're subsidizing older farmers who want to sell out and retire on their land-speculation killings, while we penalize young farmers who want to enter the business. Is that what you want to do?

(6) We'll always need what farms can produce. People won't eat less if land values were taxed.

(7) Wouldn't farmers be better off if the economy improved and their customers had more money?

(8) If the private ownership of land rent is unethical, it's unethical for farmers, too.

But there are some legitimate actions we can take for farmers:

(1) We could exempt about $1,000 per acre of farmland assessments from taxation in order to roughly reimburse them for the in-land improvements they make, such as grading, fertilizing, tree-breaking,

ponding, and fencing. The values of these in-land improvements are often wrongfully included in the land assessment.

(2) We could make it easier for farmers to pay their LRT bills by tax-billing them after harvest time when their income peaks.

(3) We could index their LRT bills to farm prices or production.

(4) Farmland could be zoned for agricultural use only.

(5) Farmers could get bad-weather insurance.

Pro-Environment

At first thought, it might seem that LRT would lead to the premature development of land, but a little examination contradicts that. In fact the environment cannot be adequately protected without LRT. Consider:

(1) **Philosophical Similarity** – Both LRT advocates and environmentalists stress that land is a gift of God or Nature to humankind and is different than human-produced goods and services.

(2) **Zoning Protection** – The best way to protect buildings of special historical or aesthetic quality is to zone them for their special use. Their underlying land value would then be zero and so such buildings would be unaffected by LRT and would be protected from profit-seeking demolition. No one, for instance, wants to see the White House demolished to make way for a profitable use. But with zoning, that needn't happen.

Zoning can protect areas that should be reserved for open space, but zoning restrictions are too often broken by profit-seekers – if they can break those restrictions, their land value will shoot up precipitously and they could profit greatly. But LRT takes the profit out of such down-zoning.

Non-land taxation is a sprawl machine. Without a doubt, LRT should be supplemented by adequate land-use controls.

(3) **LRT Can Contain Urban Sprawl** - Our cities are more porous than at first might be realized; for instance, a 1971 study in the journal *Land Economics* revealed that in the average U.S. city of more than 100,000 population, 21% of the land area was vacant yet buildable upon. Add to that the land area that was developed only

partially – i.e., it contained improvements that were not the highest-and-best use of their site. LRT would lead to urban infill and would stop sprawl into suburban and rural areas.

If urban land is not developed efficiently, then the clean-and-green countryside will be developed prematurely. If families cannot find satisfactory living space in our cities, they're forced out to the countryside; in addition, they'll live on a much larger land area than they would have in the cities.

If we green our cities, we must necessarily blacktop our countryside – goodbye then to farming and open space. But let's not ignore rural sprawl: it eats into open space. Good environmental practice requires even rural land to be used efficiently.

If you don't urge LRT, you abet urban and rural land sprawl and hurt the environment.

(4) **LRT Promotes Public Transportation.** To be profitable, public transportation requires concentration of population. LRT will promote such concentration. If the population is spread out, public transportation can never be profitable and will require huge subsidies.

Public transportation steeply increases land prices around its stations. A land value tax could fund its entire cost. Why should taxpayers enrich land speculators?

(5) **Absentee Landownership Would End** – Absentee landowners are usually bad land stewards because they're generally more interested in a rental income than in good environmental practices. But LRT would tax away their land rent, causing absentee landownership to disappear. The land would soon come under the ownership of the actual land user, who is usually more interested in good environmental practice.

(6) **LRT – A Good Revenue Source for Environmental Programs** – Such programs often are expensive; LRT could provide a logical and plentiful source of revenue for such programs.

Anti-Terrorism

"Surely, LRT has nothing to do with terrorism," some might think. "Only guns and tanks can successfully combat suicidal terrorism."

Not so. Guns and tanks are needed in the short run, but in the long run, democracy must take root if religious extremism is to be successfully combated. But only LRT can ensure democracy by abolishing poverty. Only a life-enhancing rationalism can provide an alternative to death-inviting terrorism.

Let's discuss these ideas one at a time.

(1) Guns and tanks – This book makes no pretense at offering expertise on military matters; if you thought it did, you are reading the wrong book. Since terrorists use military weapons, they must be countered militarily. But we fool ourselves if we think that in the long run, the terrorist genie can be forced back in the bottle by guns and tanks only. The root causes of terrorism will have to be removed.

Killing terrorists to get rid of them is a bad joke. That's what they want – martyrdom and eternal life with 72 maidens. Trying to kill terrorists is like trying to kill cockroaches; the terrorists have too many nests, too many supporters. Yes, we need guns and tanks to contain them, but that can be only a stopgap measure.

(2) Abolishing Poverty – If you've come this far in the book, you know how LRT can do this. But it has particular application in countries with underdeveloped economies where poverty is deep and pervasive - where labor is poorly paid and land is oil-rich.

Today, neither suicidal terrorists nor their supporters can find suitable this-world non-terrorist economic opportunities. Free enterprise as usually preached is inadequate to the task. Only LRT can make it work.

It is positively irrational to preach that all people are equal but some are to have more access to nature than others.

Is democracy *provably* correct? The answer is a resounding *yes*. For a full answer, see *Society at the Crossroads*. If democracy can't be proven, then suicidal terrorism is a reasonable alternative. The terrorists are willing to ram planes into buildings, and if we can't prove democracy then all we can say is - they're not nice. A weak response... But ultimately, democracy rests on prosperity for all, which only LRT can ensure.

True, some of the terrorists come from middle-class backgrounds, but most of them have a dim economic future. Besides, they are affronted by the poverty all around them and they want to lead their countrymen away from it. A middle-class mentality is especially susceptible to a revolutionary social program; relativism can only be a weak response to it.

Organizing terrorism takes some money and takes some schooling, for which middle and upper class terrorists are needed. There are no social movements in history that weren't led by middle-class intellectuals. But we will never eradicate terrorism and democratize the Middle East unless we tax land rent.

It is a central doctrine of suicidal terrorists that rationality can never prove anything ethical (this was the Great Secret of the 32nd degree of the medieval Order of Assassins). To oppose them successfully, everyone must have equal access to nature.

"22 Arab countries, taken together, have a smaller GNP than that of Spain alone," even despite their oil (Reader's Digest, 9/03, p. 138).

The phenomenally higher birth rate among terrorist-oriented countries lends additional urgency to this analysis. Here's what Fouad Ajami, a professor at Johns Hopkins University, writes in the *Wall Street Journal*, 3/22/04 (A18):

"Demographers tell us that the fertility replacement rate is 2.1 children per woman. Europe is frightfully below this level; in Germany it is 1.3, Italy 1.2, Spain 1.1, France 1.7 (this higher rate is a factor of its Muslim population). Fertility rates in the Islamic world are altogether different: they are 3.2 in Algeria, 3.4 in Egypt and Morocco, 5.2 in Iraq and 6.1 in Saudi Arabia."

These rates do not bode well for the future of democracy. They can be reversed only by prosperity (which not only makes democracy possible but also inhibits child-bearing). By this time you must know what is needed in the long run to engender prosperity, and therefore democracy.

We have already pointed out that land is very expensive in the Middle East (because of oil). Tax it and enrich the multitudes of desperately poor citizens; then they're more likely to stop supporting terrorists.

Bonus

If the analysis in this book is correct, then American foreign policy should try to spread LRT. In fact, shouldn't that be every nation's prime interest?

This would give the United States a sense of high purpose that it has not enjoyed since the nineteenth century. Yes, it's good to advocate peace and democracy even at the cost of occasionally being an international policeman, but these desirable goals are no longer uniquely American and will not succeed in the long run without the justice and continuous prosperity that LRT alone can promise.

An LRT-less democracy was once a great reform, back in the eighteenth century when the powers-that-were went around in knee britches and powdered hair, non-working nobles were the enemy of progress, and the divine right of kings was the dominant ideology. Democracy was certainly better than the divine right of kings and landowning nobles.

But an LRT-less democracy won't suffice for our time; to many in the world it now seems faintly passé. They ask, "Wouldn't a benevolent dictatorship be more efficient?"

It's been about two centuries since democracy was triumphing and Beethoven wrote the triumphal Ode to Joy into his Ninth Symphony. Something more is now needed. We need to complete the vision of liberty and equality for all, and the only way to do it is with LRT. It's up to us. America (or any country) can take the lead in doing this.

We all realize that the world would be a safer place if justice and prosperity reigned. The apparent need for foreign aid would be much less; it is in any case totally inadequate to combat poverty in the less developed countries. You might as well try to empty the Atlantic Ocean with a teaspoon.

An ancillary benefit: excessive immigration from Mexico would be stemmed if that country adopted LRT.

Europe is certainly not exempt from economic problems. Quoting the *Investor's Business Daily* (11/9/04, A14): "It has high tax rates, 35-hour workweeks and aging populations [we would add 'high land values']. It's no longer having enough babies to support its future welfare state. So it must import workers – the U.N. estimates about 1.35 million a year – from abroad to keep the whole thing going. Most will have to be Muslim."

Anyone starting to read this book at this point will regard all this as gross exaggeration, but is it not the logical conclusion from the ethics and evidence? If you encounter critics, be sure they present ethical logic and empirical evidence for their point of view.

We ought not expect the world's dispossessed and desperate to tolerate poverty and injustice forever. To counter these evils, America's foreign policy (and that of all nations) must embrace land rent taxation.

"It is not the Almighty but we who are responsible for the vice and misery that fester amid our civilization. The Creator showers upon us His gifts – more than enough for all. But like swine scrambling for food, we tread them in the mire – tread them in the mire, while we tear and rend each other!"

5

This chapter list over 200 well-known historical personages as well as lesser-known politicians who have actually administered land value taxation.

Several brief quotations from these endorsers are featured, including those of eight American winners of the Nobel Prize in economics.

Chapter **5**

Many Prominent Endorsers

As you might expect, LRT has attracted many enthusiastic endorsers – prominent historical personalities like presidents, prime ministers and popes, also urbanologists and city officials – so many, in fact, that the question naturally arises: if they endorsed the idea, why did they not get it adopted? There are at least three answers to this question:

(1) They had other interests

(2) They didn't cite empirical studies, just their opinions

(3) They didn't know how to implement the tax in the foreseeable future. Any diligent reader of this book's appendix will know more about how to apply LRT than did they.

At least, their endorsement of the principle which this book advocates have made it easier to obtain some partial adoptions (the results being *always* favorable).

Over the years, I have published quotations (with sources) from almost all of them, plus many more endorsements not printed here. My files contain still more endorsements, and there are many more I am unaware of. Don't overlook the wisdom of the ages. Here is a partial list of these endorsers as well as some quotations from their writings:

City/County Officials - Newton D. Baker (ex-mayor of Cleveland), Joseph Barr (ex-mayor of Pittsburgh), Russell Conklin (ex-mayor, Gt. Falls), James Clarkson (ex-mayor, Southfield MI), Tom L. Johnson (ex-mayor, Cleveland), report of 13 rural municipal or county councils in Australia, Allentown, Pa. city council study, Councilman Gavan Oakley (v.p., Aus. Municipal Assn.), Ken Synett (ex-mayor, Marion, Aus.), Sydney Aus. city council (1966 report), Michael Albert (ex-Douglas County Board Chairman, Neb.), Ralph Perk (ex-mayor, Cleveland), W. Magee (ex-mayor, Pittsburgh), John McCulloch, (ex-Chief Assessor, Johannesburg), Councilman Bennett Rodgers (Pittsburgh), Wilmington City Council (1969 study), Wm. Coyne (ex-Finance Chairman, Pittsburgh), and many more.

> **"In the development process, both the expenditures of government on infrastructure and the growth of the economy will cause land values to rise. Landowners will enjoy a benefit that has not resulted from their own investment or effort. Such windfall gains are an appropriate object of taxation. Revenue is raised, income is redistributed, while economic decisions are not distorted."**
> *- Maxwell School, Syracuse University,*
> *1986 report of the Jamaica Tax Structure Examination Project*

Philosophers & Historical Figures - Mortimer Adler, Robt. Andelson (ex-Professor of Philosophy, Auburn University), Charles A. Beard (historian), Louis D. Brandeis (ex-Supreme Court Justice), Nicholas Murray Butler (ex-President, Columbia University), Sir Henry Campbell-Bannerman, Herbert Asquith, Lord Snowden (ex-British Prime Ministers), Theodore Roosevelt, Winston Churchill, FDR ("I believe that Henry George was one of the really great thinkers produced by our country"), John Dewey (philosopher), Paul Douglas (ex-U.S. Senator from Illinois),

Wm. Cobden (19c. free-trade reformer), Ecclesiastes v. 4, 5:9, Luke 4:18, Albert Einstein, *Fortune* Magazine, U.S. GAO study, Walter Heller (ex-chairman, U.S. Council of Econ. Advisers), Ebenezer Howard (father of the garden city movement), Alduous Huxley, Helen Keller, John Kieran (one-time *N.Y. Times* columnist), Abraham Lincoln, Leviticus XXV (10, 23), John Stuart Mill, U.S. Representative Henry Reuss, Judge Samuel Seabury, Herbert Spencer, Sun Yat Sen, Leo Tolstoi, Dorothy Thompson, *Wall Street Journal* (5/22/42, 3/19/69, 8/21/72, 3/4/76, 3/12/85), Woodrow Wilson, Cecil B. DeMille, Agnes DeMille, American Institute of Economic Research, *Milwaukee Sentinel* (2/4/67), *N.Y. Times* (7 editorials, 1980s), Thomas Jefferson (1785), David Lawrence (ex-Pa. governor), *Pittsburgh Post-Gazette,* Newton D. Baker, Dwight D. Eisenhower, Wm. Blackstone, Alfred Russel Wallace, Frank Lloyd Wright, George Bernard Shaw, Wm. Buckley, Michael Kinsley, Ralph Nader, Lao-Tzu.

More: John Locke, J.S. Mill, Tom Paine, Wm Penn, Francois Quesnay, James Michener, David Ricardo, Rousseau, Adam Smith, Spinoza, Voltaire, Chas. A. Beard, Mark Twain, Sun Yat-Sen, Frank Lloyd Wright, Paul Douglas, Jack Kemp, Walter Mondale, N.Y. Times (7 editorials, 1980s, and many others.

"The present land system hampers, hobbles and restricts industry."[1]

"It is quite true that the land monopoly is not the only monopoly which exists, but it is by far the greatest of monopolies. It is a perpetual monopoly, and it is the mother of all other forms of monopoly."[2]

"I have made speeches to you by the yard on the Taxation of Land Values and you know what a strong supporter I have always been of that policy."[3]

"I have taken the trouble to re-read some of these statements [about land rent taxation] quite recently and I am bound to say that...I am not at all convinced that, among my arguments in favour of the rating [taxing] of undeveloped urban land upon its true value, I employed any which were lacking in lucidity or reason."[4]

<u>Winston Churchill</u> ([1]Drury Lane Theatre, 4/20/1907; [2]Edinburgh, 7/17/1909; [3] Dundee, 7/1917; [4]House of Commons, 6/5/1928)

Church Figures – Gregory the Great (Pope), Ambrose, St. George the Great, St. John Chrystosom, Augustine, Cardinal Francis Newman,

Wm. Temple (ex-Archbishop of Canterbury), C.D. Williams (Episcopal Bishop), Pope John Paul II, Vatican II, Pope Paul VI, Pope Pius XII, Confucius, and many more.

> **St. George the Great (Pope, 590-604): "They [the Roman landowners] wrongfully think they are innocent who claim for themselves the common gift of God [the land]."** (He didn't know about LRT then.)

Others - Albert Fondy (ex-President, Pittsburgh Teachers, Union - AFL-CIO), Professor Mason Gaffney (agricultural economist), Raymond Moley (ex-economics professor, Columbia University and presidential adviser), *Business Week* ("The Coming Change in the Property Tax"), Harold S. Buttenheim (ex-editor and founder of the *American City Magazine*), Andrew Heiskell (co-chairman, Urban Coalition), John M. Kelly (Scranton, Pa. realtor), Liberal Party (U.K.), Wm. Wilcox (ex-Secretary, Pa. D.C.A.), and many more.

> **"The site [land] value tax would also be easier to administer than the existing tax on land and buildings. Because only land is being assessed, many of the complications of assessing commercial and industrial property would be removed."**
> *William H. Wilcox (Secretary, Pennsylvania Dept. of Community Affairs, testifying before the Pennsylvania Senate Finance Committee, 8/26/76).*

Urbanologists - Ray Archer (Asst. Secy, U.S. Dept. of Environment in H.U.D.), John Due (M.I.T., African tax expert), H.W. Eastwood (ex-Chief Assessor, New South Wales, Aus.), Professor (Columbia) Lowell Harriss (1973 president, Natl. Tax Assn.), Albert Hydeman, Jr. (Secretary, Pa. Dept. of Community Affairs), Intl. Union of Local Authorities (1974 report), *Labor* (1973 issue), Local Govt. Assn. (Aus.), Carl Madden (ex-Chief Economist, U.S. Chamber of Commerce), H.L.J. May (ex-Minister of Local Govt., N.Z.), New South Wales Royal Commission on Local Govt. Finance & Valuation, 1967 report), NYC Special Planning Commission - 1964 report), Pennsylvania State Planning Commission - 1978 report), E.R.A. Seligman (19 c. Columbia professor), Donald Stone (ex-professor, Carnegie-Mellon University), Karl Falk (past pres., NAHRO), Tax Foundation (10/76 report), Lester Thurow (economics professor, M.I.T.), two U.K. Land Institute studies of Whitsable, U.N. Habitat Conference (1976), U.S. Congressional Research Service, Urban

Land Institute (Research Monographs #4, #12, and #19), Robert C. Wood (former President, Univ. of Mass., also Secretary of H.U.D.), A. M. Woodruff (ex-president, U. of Hartford and real-estate appraiser), Colin Clark (ex-economics professor, Oxford University), Brevard Crihfield (ex-Executive Director, Council of State Governments), Tom Curtis (ex-Chairman, Joint Economic Committee of Congress), Richard Doyle (ex-Indiana state representative). *Financial World, Harper's Magazine* (May 1968), Dean Gillies (director of U.C.L.A.'s Real Estate Research Program), Michigan (1976 report), Ted Gwartney (real-estate assessor), James Heilbrun (real-estate tax authority, Robt. Hutchins (ex-professor and ex-president, U. of Chicago), R.W. Hewison (chief of a Toronto study), Dan. Holland (M.I.T. professor of finance), *House & Home* magazine (esp. Aug. 1960), Arthur D. Little Co. (urban consultants), Modesto CA Chamber of Commerce, Edmund Muskie (U.S. senator), N.A.R.E.B., 1974 or 1975), National Committee on Urban Problems, Dick Netzer (N.Y.U. professor, also Brookings Institution), *New Republic* (1/27/93), Omaha study (1970s), Frank Othick (U.K. Land Institute study), Pa. Bureau of Municipal Affairs, *Practical Builder,* Kaiser Committee report, Quebec report (1976), Raymond Saulnier (ex-Chrmn., Council of Econ. Advisers), Roy Stauffer (Pa. Chamber of Commerce), *Time Magazine* (5/71), Royal Commission (U.K.), Pennsylvania Economy League (1996 study), *Nation's Cities Magazine* (3/65, 3/69, 5/70), N.L.C. *Weekly* (1/22/96), *Reader's Digest* (7/62), *Life Magazine* (12/24/65), World Bank (Deininger book, 2003, ch. 4), Mayor John Norquist, *Brookings Review* (S/00), Municipal Research Center, Missouri. Fed of Teachers (AFL-CIO), P.I. Prentice (vp, Time, Inc.), Royal Commission on Local Govt. Finance (1958), Queensland Comm. of Inquiry (1960, also 1964, 1966, 1989), N.S.W. Royal Comm. (1967, 1973), N.Z. Internal Affairs Dept. Coordinating Comm., (1989), Wellington City Comm. (1989), David Zwanetz (Vice-Chairman, Phila. Asmt. Board), Carter Murdoch (NAREB Director of Research), etc.

> **"Land value taxation is a golden key to urban renewal, to the automatic regeneration of the city – and not at public expense."**
> *- Urban Land Institute Research Monograph #4, p. 28*

Environmentalists - Louis Bromfield (author), Farm Foundation (1979 report), Washington D.C. Environmental Committee, (1999), David Brunori (1998 study, also 12/3/03 study), Md. Sierra Club study, 1001 Friends of Md., Center for Policy Alternatives, Minnesota Environmental Defense Fund, Sierra Club (New Columbia Chapter), Sprawl Watch Clearinghouse, U/Md. School of Law, *Rachel's Environmental & Health*

Weekly, Canadian Institute for Environmental Law & Policy, Toward a Sustainable Chesapeake, Audubon Society, Baltimore Heritage Soc., Md. Assn. of Hsg. & Com. Dev., Wicomico River Commission, Minnesota Environmental Quality Board, Environmental Defense Fund, etc.

> **_The Sierra Club of Maryland_ gave the two-rate [LVT-oriented] property tax its highest "strongly support" rating. The Club stated that if Baltimore were to adopt this approach, "the effect would be to draw development into the city and relieve the pressure on open space land."**

We can cite hundreds more of endorsements like these, but enough is sufficient. Full quotations by most of these endorsers are to be found in each of the back issues of *Incentive Taxation* (published eight times yearly, 1974-2004). I have additional endorsements in my files.

I have managed to encounter statements of a few LRT opponents - there weren't many, none were well known or were city officials, nor did they cite relevant facts, they just gave opinions.

Even though many prominent and well-placed commentators have advocated the taxation of land values, you yourself are under no obligation to like the proposal, but you are obliged to carefully consider it.

> **8 Recent American Winners of the Nobel Prize in Economics**
>
> **Milton Friedman:** "I share your view that taxes would be best placed on the land, not on improvements."
>
> **Herbert Simon:** "Assuming that a tax increase is necessary, it is clearly preferable to impose the additional cost on land by increasing the land tax, rather than to increase the wage tax, the two alternatives open to the City [of Pittsburgh]...The average increase in tax bills of city residents will be about twice as great with a wage tax increase than with a land tax increase."
>
> **Paul Samuelson:** "Pure land rent is in the nature of a 'surplus' which can be taxed heavily without distorting production incentives or efficiency."
>
> **James Tobin:** "I think in principle it's a good idea to tax unimproved land... Theory says we should try to tax items with zero or low elasticity, and those include sites."

> **James Buchanan:** "The landowner who withdraws land from productive use to a purely private use should be required to pay higher, not lower, taxes."
>
> **Franco Modigliani:** "It is important that the rent of land be retained as a source of government revenue. Some persons who could make excellent use of land would be unable to raise money for the purchase price. Collecting rent annually provides access to land for persons with limited access to credit."
>
> **Robert Solow:** "Users of land should not be allowed to acquire rights of indefinite duration for single payments. For efficiency, for adequate revenue and for justice, every user of land should be required to make an annual payment to the local government equal to the current rental value of the land that he or she prevents others from using."
>
> **William Vickrey** (when president-elect of the American Economics Association): "It guarantees that no one dispossesses fellow citizens by obtaining a disproportionate share of what nature provides for humanity."
>
> *The endorsements of the last three Nobel Prize winners were taken from a letter dated November 7, 1990 to Mikhail Gorbachev and signed by 30 prominent U.S. economists.*

You say you've never heard of this idea? If you're not daunted by all these endorsements, see a doctor.

6

This surprisingly turned out to be an important chapter. To begin with, we should realize that Henry George deserves to be praised as the first modern exponent of the land value tax idea. He was often supremely eloquent.

I then point out what I consider to be six flaws in his presentation. It is possible to show how the land value tax can actually replace all other taxes (imagine – no taxes on production at all!) and we also can see the best way by which to enact this tax in the foreseeable future.

Wouldn't that surely inundate poverty? If every land-site would have to be efficiently used and if production were un-taxed, wouldn't unemployment (and the fear of it) disappear? It almost sounds too good to be true, but the substantiation is ample.

Chapter **6**

Henry George: Eloquent Forerunner But Not Always Correct

*When he was right, he was very very right,
but when he was wrong, he was quoted.*

No discussion of land rent taxation can be complete without reference to Henry George. He was born in Philadelphia in 1839, wrote his masterwork *Progress and Poverty* in 1879, and died in New York City in 1897. He was the first to propound the theory of LRT completely and in modern form.

His *Progress and Poverty* was profoundly eloquent and compelling. Many passages of the book rival the Bible with its elevated prose; they find no parallel in the history of the English

71

language. *Progress and Poverty* became a runaway best seller, selling in the millions; it is still available today. Workers and intellectuals the world over read it. It profoundly influenced not only the people of his time but also most of the Progressive Era reformers in the next American generation.

He was the first to propound the theory of land value taxation in a modern form, often with great eloquence. The eminent philosopher John Dewey wrote, "It would require less than the fingers of the two hands to enumerate those who, from Plato down, rank with Henry George among the world's social philosophers."

Not only did he have great influence in his own time, but he influenced many public figures in the generation after him. Wrote historian Eric F. Goldman:

"For some years prior to 1952, I was working on a history of American reform and over and over again my research ran into this fact: An enormous number of men and women, strikingly different people, men and women who were to lead America in a dozen fields of humane activity, wrote or told someone that their whole thinking had been redirected by reading Progress and Poverty in their formative years. In this respect no other book came anywhere near comparable influence, and I would like to add this word of tribute to a volume which magically catalyzed the best yearnings of our grandfathers and fathers."

George himself was a consummate public speaker and personally admirable. A small band of followers still continues his Single Tax crusade.

Today, however, *Progress and Poverty* is little read. The book is too dense for the average 21st century reader on the run; it doesn't fit the usual categories of books that sell these days (it's not a cookbook, pop-psych book, diet book, etc.). He committed some errors of omission (more than of commission). Most present-day capsule commentators stress his deficiencies rather than his validities. The trick in reading George is to discard his errors and embrace his insights.

Six Flaws

To begin with, I must acknowledge a tremendous debt to George. This book owes much to *Progress and Poverty*. His economic analysis is worth examining closely, but I think it contains six major flaws:

(1) To begin with, George certainly understood the difference between "land value taxation" and "land rent taxation" but he referred most often to land value taxation. Because he didn't carefully distinguish between the two terms, many of his critics thought that all he wanted to do was tax the selling price of land, whereas his real intention was to reduce the private collection of the annual rent of land to zero.

The word "value" is ambiguous because it could either mean land price or annual land-rental income. It is the latter that really should be taxed, hence this book uses the unambiguous term "land rent taxation" (LRT).

George often gave many people the impression that he wanted to end the private ownership of land, whereas he actually proposed only the taxation of land rent. Many people thought (and still think) he was a land nationalist, but he clearly was not.

Also, many critics think that George was opposed to the gradual imposition of the land tax, but that's not so. In Australia in 1890, he said, "People constantly talk to us as though we were proposing some great revolution, as though we were going to institute the single tax tomorrow morning before breakfast. I, for one, would like to do so. I only regret that it can't be done. This is not the way of the world. All large reforms have to be accomplished a step at a time."

(2) Important to George was his belief that in a non-LRT economy, progress necessarily breeds poverty, but this need not be. It is altogether possible that people will work harder and more imaginatively to overcome the problems caused by non-LRT-ness. In the short run, increased productivity, such as from new inventions, can overcome poverty irrespective of non-LRT, thereby temporarily averting widespread poverty.

More-than-ample statistics indicate that since George's time, the standard of living has been steadily rising in our non-LRT economy. Here is some evidence:

✓ In the last 40 years the U.S. poverty rate, according to government statistics, has decreased. What's more, when deciding who's poor, the government doesn't include housing aid, food stamps, Medicaid, or capital-gains income (*Investor's Business Daily*, 9/25/02, A16, citing U.S. Census Bureau). Nor does it include non-monetary income, such as home-grown food, that many of the rural poor enjoy.

✓ The top income-fifth of the population work 5.8 times more per week than families in the lowest income-fifth (A.I.E.R. *Research Reports*, 1/22/01, p. 12 citing an article, based on U.S. census data, by professors Wilson Mixon & Frank Stephenson in the 1/01 issue of *Ideas on Liberty*).

✓ "68% of American families now own their own home – the highest percentage on record....The vast majority of households possess color televisions (98 percent), videocassette recorders (94 percent), microwave ovens (90 percent), frost-free refrigerators (87 percent), washing machines (83 percent), and clothes dryers (75 percent). In the past decade or so, computers and cell phones have become commonplace... (*Reason magazine*, 8/02, p. 48ff).

✓ "According to Department of Labor figures, the average workweek shrank from 59 hours in 1890 to 40 hours in 1950... Average weekly hours for production workers dropped from 39 in 1960 to 34 in 2001...Since 1950 time off for holidays has doubled, to an average of 12 days a year. We've added an average of four vacation days a year...For the most part, modern work takes place in a clean, well-lit and air-conditioned environment...(*Ibid.*).

✓ "Work isn't just more pleasant. It's also safer. Occupational injuries and illnesses, as tallied by the National Safety Council, are at an all-time low of 63 per 1,000 workers. The number of Americans killed on the job has fallen to a record low of 38 per million workers, down from 87 in 1990 and 214 in 1960...(*Ibid.*).

✓ "Annual deaths per 1 million people are at an all-time low. The age-adjusted death rate has fallen by two-thirds since 1900... Gains in transportation safety have been dramatic...(*Ibid.*).

✓ "Today, having grown richer, we can afford the pollution controls that have made Pittsburgh's air sweeter than an ocean breeze..."

The *Reason* article contained much more hard evidence attesting to the disappearance of poverty and the improvement of the environment in America today.

✓ Michael Cox (sr. v.p. at the Dallas F.R.B.) and Richard Alm (a writer) found that most of those in the lowest income quintile moved up to higher quintiles in ensuing years; few remained in the lowest income quintile for long. *(Ibid.)*

✓ The Sphere Institute tracked the wages of more than 180,000 Californians from 1988 to 2000 and found that all quintiles moved up the economic ladder, and the "real wage gains were greatest for those workers who started out at the lowest wages..."

I wasn't trying very hard to amass all this evidence. I could easily amass much more; certainly in any short run, poverty can increase even with progress. George hurt his cause by making a claim that the facts can't support. We're not faced with the growth of poverty, but rather with obesity.

Poverty exists in this country, but it's not because some people are rich. There are those who say, "If people are poor, give them money." I say, "Give them opportunity."

Some of his present-day followers ascribe the general economic improvement to the effects of unions and minimum wage legislation, but that's unlikely. In the United States, unions constitute 8% (and declining) of the private workforce and many unions exert little influence. In fact, by raising prices they often increase poverty.

As for the minimum wage, only a few workers get that little, and of those who do, many lack marketable skills or are middle-class teenagers living at home. In this case, too, the minimum wage can often increase poverty by raising prices.

Nevertheless, there is too much poverty and unemployment in America and elsewhere. If we tax properly, these evils would quickly disappear.

(3) George *started* his ethical argument for LRT with an unproven conclusion - "we each own ourselves." We can agree with that, but

it is a conclusion that George should prove but he only assumed. One shouldn't base an ethical argument on an assumption, on a conclusion.

Furthermore, George relied on the natural-rights theory for ethical justification, but that theory is quite correctly held in disrepute these days. Why is nature always right? Are earthquakes right because they are natural? Dangerous bacteria are not right, even though they are natural. Nature is red in tooth and claw – is that right?

Natural law and natural rights attempt to contravene the uncontravenable Is-Ought Barrier. You cannot logically base a statement of what ought to be on what is; there is an impassable wall between the two. It is, if you will, the *pons asinorum* of ethical thinking.

Fortunately, there is a logically airtight proof of George's ethical basis for LRT that doesn't depend on natural law - see chapter two.

(4) George's explanation for depressions offers some valid insights, but ultimately it was insufficient because depressions have causes other than speculation in land. These causes are treated at length in the next chapter. Nevertheless, his emphasis on land speculation merits consideration.

Interestingly, George advocated a scheme of counter-cyclical bank borrowing to combat depression, presaging John Maynard Keynes (see HG Jr., *Life*, p. 558).

Inflation simply wasn't a problem in George's time so he said little or nothing about it, but we shouldn't do that today.

(5) Can the LRT be a Single Tax - i.e., the only tax, replacing all other taxes? George's didn't doubt that for a moment; he assumed that there was enough land rent to amply replace all taxes. But today that doesn't seem likely. Fortunately, a logical proof rather than an empirical proof can be provided.

Remember, he wrote in 1879 – taxes then were minuscule and land rent loomed large. There seemed to be no reason to doubt the singleness of the LRT. In fact, his contemporary critics worried that LRT would give the government too much revenue and lead to corruption.

But since then, taxes on producers have grown much faster than rent. Proving that LRT can be a single tax must be found other than by adding up existing land rents (anyway, it hasn't been done and can't be done).

Of course, even if it couldn't replace all other taxes, shouldn't we still replace as many taxes on production as possible with LRT? If it should be levied, then let's levy it. If LRT can be single, all well and good; if it can't, it should be levied anyway. No other tax is discarded because it can't be single.

But after I finished writing about 85% of this book, it suddenly dawned on me that if we clear up the common ambiguity concerning the word "value" in the term "land value taxation" which George himself prominently used and so did I for the last 54 years, then yes, **we can logically prove that _LRT could become a Single Tax!_** George had arrived at the right conclusion, although from inadequate reasoning.

Before you drum me out of the ranks of the sane, read me out. It certainly seems true that a tax on current land *price* could not be a Single Tax - **no, no, no, no** (nevertheless, some will interpret that as yes).

Many critics mislead themselves by considering the price of land to be the intended object of taxation, whereas actually it is the public collection of the annual land rent income. In fact, if land prices are taxed high enough, they would sink to zero and it would produce no revenue at all!

By using the ambiguous term "land value taxation" for 54 years, I misled myself. It didn't do me any good that others also made this mistake. I have now re-read all the previous chapters of this book in order to remove ambiguities.

Here's how LRT could become a Single Tax:

1 - As the LRT gradually increases, all land-sites will be used more efficiently (because the owners of productive improvements would then be more likely to outbid the owners of less productive improvements) and taxes falling on private initiative will gradually decrease. These two effects will increase the Gross Domestic Product.

2 - This GDP increase will increase the taxable land rent.

3 - The increased LRT will then increase GDP, which in turn will increase LRT, which will then increase GDP again, and so on *ad infinitum.* Expressed graphically –

In other words, LRT (gradually imposed) increases GDP, then the increased GDP increases LRT, which then increases GDP, until eventually LRT replaces all the non-LRT taxes and becomes a Single Tax. What we have here is a self-feeding loop. It certainly beggars the imagination that eventually there could be no taxes on human effort!

But it gets even better:

1) Currently, there is much privately collected land rent (often illegally under-assessed); when fully taxed, it could add to the government's revenue and can even fund an ample Citizen's Dividend payment to all its citizens (which in itself will further increase LRT).

2) Nowadays, the electro-magnetic spectrum is another natural resource that ought to be taxed like land. A lengthy detailed study of the New America Foundation estimates it is at least $800 billion in the U.S. (as of 12/31/01), which is about 12½% of estimated U.S. land values.

3) The need for government welfare will be considerably less, leaving still more revenue for a Citizen's Dividend.

Conceivably, we could be faced with a new problem: how to motivate recipients of such an ample Citizen's Dividend by creativity and altruism rather than by the fear of poverty and unemployment.

All this should not surprise you. Remember, LRT *works exactly the opposite* of all other taxes; they decrease GDP, but LRT increases it. Maybe you should re-read the section in chapter one dealing with the 14 differences between taxes on land and all other taxes (there are undoubtedly more).

Could these ideas be found in Henry George's writings? Separately yes, but he never explicitly combined the three steps leading to the self-feeding loop shown above. He felt there was enough land rent for LRT to easily replace all taxes; at the time he was living, no one doubted that. If he didn't emphasize this self-feeding loop thesis, it is because he didn't have to. That job has been left for us to do.

Since his time, land rent has increased, but it has been held back by skyrocketing non-LRT taxes. The singleness of LRT has to be proven by logic, not by unavailable facts. Keep in mind that taxable land rent will grow if non-land income is not taxed.

Consider communist Cuba. The current rent of land there is just about zero; since the government takes practically all that is produced, no one would pay much (if anything) for the right to produce. But when Cuba becomes free and the GDP increases, taxable land rent will start to increase. LRT could then become a Single Tax there.

This book has presented a mountain of logic and evidence that LRT is the most important idea ever thought of in the history of humankind and it alone can prevent the long-run disappearance of free enterprise and democracy because it can eliminate the age-old curse of poverty brought on by the taxation of human effort.

Now let the critics cavil (but insist they present hard evidence).

Without LRT, poverty and unemployment will stalk the land, leading to suffering and unhappiness. Equal rights will become a memory only. Prisons will sprout where churches should be, and ultimately free enterprise and democracy will fade away. Liberty promises much, but it cannot long be denied.

(*My advice:* when promoting LRT, be careful about mentioning its capability of being a Single Tax. Many of your listeners will think that sounds too good to be true and will automatically reject what you say, preferring sounds to facts and logic.)

6. While writing this chapter, something else very important occurred to me: even though compensation to landowners for taxing their land rent income is clearly unjust, *the non-taxation of land rent is worse;* not only is it unjust, but it creates poverty and such social problems as crime, drug use, depressions, inflation, and high taxes on production.

Steven B. Cord

Sometimes we have to choose the lesser of two evils. For instance, wouldn't it have been better and cheaper if America had freed the slaves before 1861 by compensating the slave owners for the loss of their slaves, even though it was the slaves who were morally entitled to the compensation? At least that would have avoided a terrible civil war.

(Even better, the U.S. government might have given the compensation money to the slaves directly with the proviso that they must use it to buy their freedom.)

Readers of this book should know by this time why compensation to landowners would be unjust: it would tax-burden the producers while giving money to landowners who have not produced anything. That's unjust. It would eventually lessen the Citizen's Dividend to which everyone is entitled. But since compensation would hasten the adoption of the Single Tax and the Citizen's Dividend, then it should be done.

Here's how to do this compensation scheme: the federal or state governments should issue bonds to buy the land (just the land) in a small economically depressed town at assessed market value and give the land-rent money to the town's government in place of taxes (with the proviso that public expenditure could not increase by more than 2% per year over the inflation rate).

Labor & capital would not be affected at all; they would just pay their land rent to the government instead of to private landowners. This is what would happen:

> The town's government would suffer no diminution in revenue. The taxes it had levied would be at least fully replaced by the federal or state land rent.
> The town would prosper, being tax-free with every site being efficiently used.
> The state or federal government would eventually be fully repaid as the town prospered and the assessed value of the land (and therefore its land rent) increased. Those governments might even end up making money!
> Storeowners would prosper because their local customers would have more money; they would also attract out-of-town customers because of the lower tax-free prices.

80

> ➤ <u>Employment would grow</u> – with no taxes or land prices to pay, industries would be attracted to the town, bringing in new jobs.
> ➤ <u>Homeowners</u> would have more money than they ever had before (from the land they would sell) which would more than cover their land-rent. Also, they'd benefit from the lower tax-free prices.
> ➤ <u>Tenants</u> (as tenants) would all get space-rent decreases because building taxes wouldn't be passed on to them; as consumers, they all would benefit because of the lower tax-free prices.
> ➤ <u>Absentee landowners</u> would have a bond-interest income to equal their current land rent income, especially if their land were vacant or near-vacant.

Initially, this could require about a thousandth of H.U.D.'s annual budget. (!)

Everybody would win. Any city could do this; it is the equivalent of an immediate 100% LRT. There's no need to wait until economic conditions get more desperate. It sounds almost too good to be true, but after all, a rising tide raises all boats.

What are you doing to bring this about?

Ethical analysis can point to the eventual goal but we must find the most practical way to achieve that goal. George, however, was an ethical purist - not for him an ethical compromise.

I spent more than fifty years of my life in the rational dark - I opposed compensation. I thought that all I had to do was to get American cities to shift some of their building tax to land and then do empirical studies showing that even slight shifts caused spurts in new construction and renovation. The news of these studies would then spread the idea like a grease spot in water. Surely, I thought, politicians and voters would be influenced by the facts.

I therefore induced nearly two-dozen cities to adopt this shift, and *all* my studies of them showed positive economic results. But there has been no resonance, no bandwagon effect at all. A new approach is obviously needed.

Let's be practical. Compensation could bring on LRT quickly. We don't have much time left to establish economic justice in our own country, not to mention elsewhere. The WMD terrorists are creeping up on us. It's two minutes to midnight.

A Look at History

Henry George had a considerable impact on the world's history:

1. He was the first to present the Single Tax in modern form. He was incisively right in many important ways and he was frequently eloquent.

2. His 19th century contemporaries shared his natural-law assumptions and this helped popularize him and his *Progress and Poverty.* To his contemporaries, God Himself seemed to ordain land value taxation, or at least Ethics did. People today, however, no longer embrace his worldview.

3. George's messianic fervor caused his followers to think in vast terms of social justice – "let's do it now, everywhere, without compensation, and let's appeal to the voters as did George." These followers ignore the gradual foreseeable-future steps that can lead to the eventual goal of the Single Tax. They avoid learning the necessary procedures and formulas that make implementation possible in the foreseeable future. They think too grandly.

Many Georgists today try to insert their land value tax advocacy into a contradictory green amalgam of environmentalism, libertarianism, land nationalization, liberalism, socialism, and anarchism, thereby misleading just about everyone and convincing few.

They rely too heavily on the precept, "each one tells one" – but that's not the way LRT is going to spread. Politicians are easier to reach than voters – there are fewer of them than voters and if they implement the tax, then the voters will show interest.

A close friend of George's, Judge James Maguire (later a congressman), was one day walking down a street in San Francisco when he came upon a large crowd in front of a store window, gawking at a picture of a rather ordinary landscape. When he asked a bystander what was so remarkable about the picture, he was told that it was a picture of a huge cat.

Maguire exclaimed that try as he might, he saw no cat, but then suddenly he saw it (he was looking at a double picture) and ever afterward all he could see in the picture was the cat. Soon, "seeing the cat" became an expression of Georgists for describing their view of the economy at large – only the land rent tax (the cat) was to be seen while the economy (the larger picture) was obscured.

To conclude: Henry George is to be commended for eloquently expounding the case for LRT. He was the first in history to present it so completely and eloquently, but his analysis was less than perfect and it led to LRT being ignored in our time. We have to correct his shortcomings.

The triumph of Liberty and Rationalism ought not to be long delayed, otherwise there will be a terrible price to be paid.

7

The usual anti-depression and anti-inflation explanations will never be fully satisfactory unless this book's proposal is taken into account.

Taxes on production and the inefficient use of land-sites during a period of prosperity lead to depression, and a depression (or the fear of it) leads to excessive reliance on inflation. Both of these economic problems can be eliminated with this book's main proposal.

Our country is burdened with a great deficit and faces a much greater one in the near future. The proposal put forth in this book can lighten it. Thus, this chapter deals with current economic problems.

Chapter 7

Countering Depressions & Inflations

No one wants to see a return of the Great Depression of the 1930s. Everyone, conservative and liberal alike, regard it as a fearful ever-present spectre. It underlies our economic thinking, as if it happened yesterday, not many decades ago. Even an unrelenting inflation is preferred to a terrible depression.

Can LRT counter depressions and inflations? Yes, but we must not ignore other relevant factors.

Let's start with depressions first. Obviously, if we tax producers more, we can tip the economy into a depression. This could also occur if we tax land rent less - then land-sites won't be used efficiently and less will be produced on them; that's depressionary.

But there's something else: un-taxed land prices can escalate because new locations can't be produced to restrain land-price increases resulting from future expectations – i.e., the hope of selling land at a higher price in the future instead of developing it now. This is called land speculation and it can make production unprofitable and bring on a depression.

Speculation in labor & capital doesn't have that disadvantage because it causes an increase in supply (not a decrease as with speculation in land), thereby negating any speculative effect on prices.

In recent years the once-high-flying Japanese economy was mired in a deep recession, if not an actual depression. Why so? Bad bank loans, but those loans were based on land speculation. Eventually, the land speculation collapsed (not after land taxation but after much suffering) and the economy finally revived.

Depressions reduce land prices, bringing them into consonance with economic reality and enable production to resume; but LRT can do that without a depression by removing the profit from land speculation. An LRT-less economy invites depression.

A minor incident, such as a rumor, tax increase (Smoot-Hawley comes to mind), failure of a banking house, a scandal, an OPEC price hike, etc. can abruptly topple the economy into a full-scale depression. It's like stretching a rubber band until it suddenly snaps and breaks. These minor incidents can be the initiating causes of a depression, but they're not the underlying cause. Land speculation could be.

The ensuing depression reduces the land speculation, thereby unburdening labor & capital and enabling them to start producing again. The economy revives, but in the absence of LRT a new land speculation begins again. The whole boom-and-bust process is repeated, but not if we take the profit out of land speculation by instituting LRT.

That's what Henry George maintained; very neat. It's all true enough as far as it goes, but we must not overlook the other causes of depression that can be independent of land speculation. Here's a partial list of them:

➢ Consumer and investor demand can decline; there's no reason to expect it will remain constant
➢ Producer efficiency may decline
➢ The pace of invention may decline

➢ So also may the propensity to save
➢ Oil is important to our economy but it is produced in unstable parts of the world and its availability can be unpredictably curtailed
➢ The supply of money can suddenly decrease
➢ Monopoly and unions may start burdening the active producers more than previously
➢ The rate of crime may increase, deterring production
➢ Wars and terrorism could cause a depression
➢ A surge in new government taxation or regulations can send the economy into a depressionary tail-spin
➢ A bumbling leader can undermine the mood of the country or a confidence-inspiring leader can strengthen it
➢ Natural disasters such as droughts, floods, hurricanes and earthquakes can bring on a depression.

The government is rather powerless to remove these non-LRT causes of depression, except that it can counter a decrease in the money supply by increasing it, thereby maintaining spending and keeping the economy going.

It might be asked, "doesn't the money-supply increase cause prices to rise, thereby deterring consumers and investors from buying?" Eventually yes, but not in the short run if the newly created money allows consumers and investors to start buying again, thereby averting a depression. The government hopes to reduce the money supply in the next economic period, thus avoiding inflation.

Counter-Cyclical Government Bank-Borrowing

There are two ways by which the government can increase the money supply:

(1) It can print new money and reduce taxation when a depression threatens. Consumers and investors would then have more money to spend the economy out of the threatening depression. The new money can be withdrawn from circulation when prosperity returns.

But government officials don't trust themselves to do this – it is too seductively easy to run the printing presses overtime and print more money than the economy needs. This would be inflationary.

Increasing taxes while destroying some of the tax receipts is difficult for politicians to do.

(2) Instead, government officials prefer to borrow money from banks in order to counter a depression because banks have the ability to create new money seemingly out of thin air; technically, this is called counter-cyclical government bank-borrowing (C-C G B-B). But this requires some explanation.

If the government were to *borrow* from consumers and investors, it would have more money to spend to keep the economy going but then consumers and investors would have less money. There'd be no net gain in purchasing power and the economy would still be mired in depression.

But when the government borrows money from the banks, the result is different.

The banks are rarely fully loaned out; they can almost always safely lend more money to the government because they know from experience that only a few depositors withdraw money from their accounts on any given day (not counting runs on the banks, which doesn't happen often) so generally the banks can safely set up new accounts for the government. Eventually, the banks will be repaid.

When the government takes up the unused lending capacity of the banks, it gets money to spend on various make-work projects in order to counter the depression. Of course, the government eventually has to pay back what it has borrowed from the banks. But when the government spends more than it receives in taxes, it must go into deficit.

But governments have found that they have to constantly issue more money than had existed previously in order to jolt the economy out of depression; this is inflationary. The result is chronic inflation.

Franklin D. Roosevelt inherited a serious depression when he became president, but from 1932 to 1939 (peacetime years) prices were inflated by a mere 1.92%, not nearly enough to restore prosperity. In World War II, prices were inflated by 29.26% (source: U.S. govt. statistics) and that was enough to enough to counter the depression.

Since then, we've been willing to endure chronic inflation in order to avoid a depression. In 1939, just before World War II, the U.S. price level was roughly equivalent to that of 1790, but from 1939 to 2004, with counter-cyclical government bank-borrowing – also known as Keynesianism after its progenitor, John Maynard Keynes - U.S. prices grew about 13 times *(Ibid.)*

The Keynesian approach for countering depressions requires government deficits, which have often been huge. But rather than going into deficit and inviting inflation, the U.S. government would have done better to have lowered taxes on production in order to give consumers and investors more money to get the economy going again, even if the revenue shortfall had to be met by having the government go into deficit.

That could have gotten the country out of depression. Instead, FDR chose to increase government spending (In his defense, he was faced with a real crisis - people had been unemployed for months, even years, and many were near starvation; he had to find jobs in a hurry, so he established the CCC, WPA, NRA, etc.)

Both approaches have an anti-depression effect, but lowering taxes is more desirable than increased government spending. No doubt, FDR's predecessor, Herbert Hoover, should have utilized it. A government deficit is not desirable but it's better than depression.

But the most desirable anti-depression approach of all would have utilized LRT. If LRT had been used, the resulting government deficit would have been much smaller.

Let us now focus more on what to do about inflation. Don't make light of it – by raising prices, it is particularly hard on poor consumers. It raises the cost of being poor and a government deficit is clearly inflationary.

Interestingly, conservatives are now embracing Keynesianism, however much they have disliked Keynes personally. As Richard Nixon asserted, "we're all Keynesians now." To counter an unacceptable depression, they have been willing to have the government go into deficit.

Liberals may admire Keynes personally but now seem more concerned about the size of the government deficit. But their concern, as I write, is likely to be only temporary.

Any discussion of the inflation stemming from C-C G B-B would not be complete unless we consider its five drawbacks:

(1) Once consumers and investors start factoring in future price inflation, more and more inflation will be required before they'll start buying as previously. We could eventually suffer from both depression and inflation.

(2) This approach benefits borrowers at the expense of lenders, which is not likely to be just.

(3) It becomes seductively easy for politicians to fund wild spending schemes with bond-buying deficits. Present-day voters get government services that their children will eventually have to pay for.

(4) The inflation rate can change unpredictably, thereby making planning difficult for producers.

(5) Inflation undermines all standards, not only economic ones. When the monetary unit is no longer a constant measure of economic value, then everything else starts to seem changeable and fluid; nothing seems certain. Ethical relativism is promoted and general morals decline.

LRT can improve the performance of C-C G B-B in these ways:

o   It will abolish land speculation that causes increases in both the price of land and the general price level. By removing the land-speculation cause of depressions, it can reduce the need for price-increasing C-C G B-B.

o   Producers must include non-LRT taxes in their prices, thereby further inflating prices. But LRT would remedy that (remember, land taxes never boost prices while all other taxes do).

In order to avoid economic downturns, we will need both LRT and C-C G B-B (but the need will be less).

In order to counter depressions and inflation, LRT might yet be resorted to - if the readers of this book *act* to support it. It could happen; you never know. History and footballs take unforeseen bounces. There's hope for democracy and free enterprise yet.

8

During a career covering many years, these are the 63 objections I have most frequently encountered. I have tried to answer them succinctly here.

The format of this chapter is somewhat unusual.

Chapter **8**

Objections and Replies

Let's do things a little differently in this chapter. Listed here are some of the most cogent objections I've heard in my many years of LRT advocacy, followed by what I think are appropriate replies. You be the judge.

xxxxxxxxxxxxxxxxxxxxxxxxxxxxxxxxxxxxxxxxxxxxxxxxxxxxxxxxxxx
xxxxxxxxxxxxxxxxxxxxxxxxxxxxxxxxxxxxxxxxxxxxxxxxxxxxxxxxxxx

Ethics

Objection: *"Shouldn't landowners be taxed like everyone else?"*
Reply: No, because as landowners they don't produce anything, so tax them and not the active producers, labor & capital. The latter two shouldn't have to share what they produce with non-producers.

Neither landowners nor slaveowners produce anything (as landowners or slaveowners), so tax away their ill-gotten gains.

Objection: *"Shouldn't everyone be taxed equally?"*
Reply: No. Wouldn't it be wrong for everyone to be robbed equally? We shouldn't be taxed on what we produce, only on the value of the natural resources we have access to. Those resources should be equally available to us all.

Objection: *"I could buy land, so am I not entitled to use it as I wish, to sell it for a profit or to get rent for it?"*
Reply: You would be entitled to develop it, yes, but to keep the rent, no. Buying shares of a monopoly doesn't justify monopoly, does it? You could buy a slave, but that wouldn't justify slavery. You could buy stolen goods, but all you bought was a bum ethical title. Only things made by labor are ethically ownable.

Objection: *"Doesn't the law allow the private ownership of land rent?"*
Reply: Generally it does, but that only makes it legally right. There is a higher law that we appeal to when we criticize legal laws, as we all do occasionally. That higher law is the ethical law according to which the private ownership of land rent is wrong. The legal law should conform to the higher ethical law, not vice versa."

Objection: *"Why do you hate landowners?"*
Reply: I don't. I just hate landrentowning.

Objection: *"Don't the Dutch create land when they build polders?"*
Reply: No, they merely rearrange dirt; building owners do the same when they build. Land isn't just dirt, its location and neither the Dutch nor anyone else create locations.

Objection: *"Sometimes the government charges a fee based on services rendered, as when the government cleans a beach, maintains its waterline, and provides lifeguards. Wouldn't such fees be just?"*
Reply: Yes, the government could legitimately charge for those services and supplement its LRT income with those fees. But it shouldn't force taxpayers to pay for services they don't want.

Objection: **"Landowners perform a real service by collecting the land rent. They ought to be repaid for this service."**

Reply: Agreed. But rent collectors ordinarily get only 2% or 3% of the rent collected, not all of it.

Objection: **"Shouldn't we tax the efficient to subsidize the inefficient? Shouldn't we tax those who have so we can subsidize poverty?"**

Reply: No.

Objection: **"Landowners are often smart and take risks, for which they ought to be rewarded."**

Reply: "No. Smartness and risk-taking don't *justify* an income; only labor does. Crooks, monopolists and slaveowners might also be smart and take risks."

Objection: **"It's certainly true that new land can't be produced to meet demand, but it can be used more intensively, which is the same thing."**

Reply: No, it's not the same thing either ethically or economically:

(1) Ethically: intensity of use has nothing to do with whether or not the income from a site is *justified.* A monopoly may use its property intensively, but that doesn't justify monopoly (or slavery).

2) Economically: what you say is irrelevant. If some land is underused, then other lands will be used more intensively, but that is irrelevant economically. If all land rent is taxed fully, then *all* land sites will be used more intensively.

Objection: **"Some developers create land value, as did Bill Levitt who built Levittown after World War II on what had been Long Island potato fields. Developers like him rightfully own the land values they created, and their heirs can inherit that right."**

Reply: Not so. Society created that value so it should own it. Levitt merely recognized that value before anyone else. When someone makes a location, let me know.

Objection: *"We shouldn't change the rules in the middle of the game."*

Reply: That may be true for games, but not for society. Are we never to improve society by instituting social improvements gradually? People are suffering because productive effort is being taxed instead of land rent. You don't want to change that?

Objection: *"Wasn't Oliver Wendell Holmes correct when he said that taxes are what we pay for living in a civilized society?"*

Reply: Yes, but taxes should be correctly levied, as on land rent and not on production. We shouldn't be forced to pay for both land and for public services.

Objection: *"Aren't first settlers entitled to own the land they found – and therefore aren't their heirs and assigns entitled to own it? After all, the first settlers put their labor into the land."*

Reply: Not so: they only found a piece of what belongs to everyone – i.e., the earth, the land. It's not like finding a coin whose owner can't be found. But practicality requires that land be privately owned, so the law should allow private land ownership as long as the land's annual income (land rent) is taxed.

Anyway, the first settlers didn't put their labor into the land – at best, they put it into a crop. They put their labor *onto* the land. Many of the first claimers were land speculators - what rights could they legitimately claim?

No one (first settlers included) ever created land. God or nature did that a number of years ago.

Objection: *"Landowners contribute their land to the productive process, so they are entitled to a return."*

Reply: No, only labor can *justify* ownership, not mere contribution. Slaveowners contribute the labor of their slaves to the productive process, but that doesn't justify slavery. Thieves and monopolists also contribute, but not justly.

Objection: *"Should I feel guilty if I own land?"*

Reply: No, only if you collect land rent. Work to down-tax labor & capital and up-tax landrentowning.

Objection: *"Land by itself has no ability-to-pay, and so it should not be taxed. But a building has ability-to-pay, so it should be taxed."*

Reply: Taxation should be based on access to nature's opportunities, not on the ethical standard of a thief, which is ability-to-pay.

Objection: *"Taxes are for benefits received. At least we get government services in return."*

Reply: When the government collects tolls to pay for a bridge, OK, motorists voluntarily use the bridge and have received a benefit; they could choose not to use the bridge, so the toll could be conceived as a benefit received.

But taxes are mandatory for all of us, even if we don't want the benefits they fund. If a car salesman points a gun at us and says, "Buy this car or die," we'd object and rightfully so; we may not want the car (or the government services) forced on us, or pay the price the car salesman (or the government) deems proper.

Non-LRT taxes violate our private property rights; other people get to share our income and wealth. I get to share theirs, but the exchange is not likely to be equal and it certainly won't be just. Down with robbery, even mutual robbery.

Objection: *"Isn't stock-market speculation morally equivalent to land speculation?"*

Reply: No - corporate stock is a product of labor and is therefore morally ownable.

If something has been produced by labor, then it can be morally owned. Stock ownership meets that criterion; land-rent ownership doesn't.

Objection: *"President Reagan said that whatever you tax, you get less of."*

Reply: Wrong – if you tax land, you won't get less of it. The earth won't shrink. In fact, if you tax land values or land rent, more land will be used and used more fully.

__Objection:__ "Taxing land values – it's too good to be true."
__Reply:__ Present evidence. No further comment.

xxxxxxxxxxxxxxxxxxxxxxxxxxxxxxxxxxxxxxxxxxxxxxxxxxxxxxxxxxx

Economics

__Objection:__ "You want government ownership of the land – that's socialism."
__Reply:__ No, I don't want government ownership of the land. I have made that repeatedly clear. But taxes on labor & capital – that's real socialism - the government owns a little bit of each of us, so do away with such taxes.

__Objection:__ "Isn't land just like any other commodity?"
__Reply:__ No, it is strictly limited in supply and no one made it – just the reverse for human-produced goods and services. Taxes on production deter production and jobs while LRT spurs production and jobs.

__Objection:__ "Land isn't very important in our economy these days."
__Reply:__ In 2003, annual land rents were about double corporate after-tax profits. And if produced goods and services were un-taxed, then those rents would be much higher.

__Objection:__ "Vacant land produces no income, so why should it be taxed?"
__Reply:__ The owner is keeping a valuable economic opportunity out of use, thereby hurting others unjustly (even if unintentionally) and causing labor & capital to be taxed. If the land's value is taxed, the owner would be motivated to develop it or sell it to someone who would develop it (without tax penalty, be it noted), thereby creating jobs and general prosperity for all.

Objection: *"The income tax is more of an ability-to-pay tax than is LRT."*

Reply: Not so because most everyone has an income, but few have a significant land-rent income.

Anyway, ability-to-pay is an unjust standard: why should we tax ability? Is something wrong with ability that we should tax it? Karl Marx said, "from each according to his ability" – that's like the highwayman saying, "Stand and deliver."

But as it happens, LRT is more of an ability-to-pay tax than even the income tax (which, it may surprise you to know, is no longer even the federal government's chief revenue source). And if we were to use the LRT alleviations mentioned in this book, it would be even more of an ability-to-pay tax.

In 1979, a study by Anthony Pileggi, then a student at Indiana University of Pennsylvania but now a lawyer in Columbia, Md., found that 1.5% of the biggest landowners in Indiana, Pa., a town of 15,001 population, paid 53.5% of the property tax on land values, but in that year the top 3% of income earners in the U.S. paid 30.6% of the federal income tax. LRT is more likely to be an ability-to-pay tax in towns larger than Indiana, Pa. There are a number of other studies reaching this same conclusion.

Objection: *"Some property owners will pay more property tax if we adopt two-rate."*

Reply: Some will - a minority; their increase will generally be small compared to their total income and they will enjoy a better local business climate as a result of the new tax. Most "pay-mores" are likely to be absentee landowners who have an income flow that will make it easier for them to pay an increase.

But to fully protect landowners, we should introduce the new tax system gradually. An LRT law should provide that no property owner need pay more than 3% or 5% in addition to the official B.L.S. inflation rate above what was paid in the previous year because of a rate (not assessment) increase. That's more protection than landowners have now.

Objection: _"Won't LRT worsen parking problems in a city?"_
Reply: No:
1) Parking lots should be located on back and side streets, where the LRT is quite moderate.
2) Multi-level garages provide much good parking, and they generally save if locations are taxed more than structures. One way to hamstring a downtown is to strew parking lots on office-building sites.

Objection: _"Why do you favor the property tax?"_
Reply: I absolutely oppose the property tax as it is currently structured. I want to abolish the property tax on buildings, for all the reasons I have spent this whole book explaining. Property = land + buildings. Just gradually tax the first and un-tax the second.

Objection: _"Landowners will go bankrupt if they have to pay a higher land rent tax for a site for which there is no current market."_
Reply: If there is no current market for a site, that site's market value should be zero, so should its assessment and LRT. Landowners won't have any trouble paying that.

The over-assessment of land can hurt landowners, yes, but then correcting the over-assessment is the obviously correct remedy.

Objection: _"Why should landowners fill in their land-sites if it increases the value of their site, causing them to pay a higher tax?"_
Reply: They would be fully protected if they receive a credit for land-value increases due to their needed landfill.

Here's what can be done: landowners should register their landfills with the assessor. If the land is assessed at $100,000 now but is assessed for $10,000 more in the next re-assessment of which $2,000 is due to general land price appreciation in the neighborhood, then that landfill is worth $8,000 ($10,000 - $2,000) and the landowner should get a credit for that amount.

Objection: *"It doesn't matter what you tax – consumption, income, payroll, sales, land – it's all the same. We end up paying all taxes."*

Reply: No, it matters. All taxes produce revenue, but beyond that, whatever you say about taxes on what has been produced, the exact *opposite* is true of taxes on land rent: Tax anything that is humanly produced and you reduce its supply (and increase its price). But not so with land - it is fixed in supply; a tax on it can't reduce it.

Taxing land produces more wealth and opportunity, not less.

Objection: *"Speculation is desirable."*

Reply: Labor & capital speculation is desirable. For instance, grain speculation can lead to higher grain prices, which will call forth more grain production, thereby ending the speculation.

But speculation in land can't do that because new land can't be created. In fact, just the reverse: when landowners speculate, they keep land out of full use; there's actually *less* land available for production. If land assessments were taxed at a higher rate, land speculation would become unprofitable and we could down-tax buildings and other things.

A land rent tax has effects exactly opposite all other taxes. Tax location, not production (i.e., don't tax goods & services).

Objection: *"Isn't a wide tax base better than a narrow one, and doesn't that make a building-and land property tax better than a land-only property tax base?"*

Reply: A wide tax base is certainly better than a narrow one, but that advantage is small compared to the advantages of a land tax. Taxing personal property provides an even wider tax base, but it's not desirable. Taxing all human effort is wider still, but don't do it.

Objection: *"An empty lot doesn't use government services and thus shouldn't pay a property tax. But buildings get government services and so their owners should pay for those services. For example, buildings get fire protection from a fire department (land doesn't burn) and so should be taxed to pay for that protection."*

Reply: Government services, such as fire protection, make the location more valuable, so tax it to pay for those services. Then you won't have to tax buildings.

As for fire-traps, outlaw them.

Objection: *"We're already all built up. We don't have much vacant land."*

Reply: Is your locality perfect? Unimprovable? Every locality should encourage private enterprise to maintain and improve its buildings. No locality is all built up forever. Don't wait until your locality is dilapidated before you act to improve it.

Besides, there is more vacant land than most people realize. They just don't notice it.

Objection: *"If we impose a tax on land value, we'll make it too expensive to own land or develop it."*

Reply: No, just the opposite. See the empirical studies in chapter three, and I can send you 215 more such studies. How many empirical studies do you have? Both land prices and rent will drop.

Objection: *"Property taxes are not important in decisions to develop sites."*

Reply: Not so – in Detroit, for instance, the capitalized tax on buildings is equivalent to 72% of the construction cost of a new building.

There are hundreds of empirical studies showing that down-taxing buildings and up-taxing land creates new construction and renovation.

Objection: ***"In leasehold situations, the land is owned by leaseholders, the building by others; the leaseholders would be taxed into bankruptcy."***

Reply: No, in most leasehold situations now, property taxes are paid by the building owner. In any case, leaseholders should have an option to buy the building.

Objection: *"I've heard that property-tax abatements don't result in more construction."*

Reply: "You've heard" – n.g., cite specific studies. Chapter two contains 22 empirical studies, all showing good economic results from LVT. And there are 215 more such studies. *215!* How many do you have?

Anyway, property-tax abatements lower the tax rate on land assessments; only the building tax should be abated.

Objection: ***"LRT is a good idea, but it can't do much good."***

Reply: I notice you don't cite any specific evidence. But this book presents a mountain of evidence proving that LRT results in new construction and renovation. In addition, there are my own 18 studies and probably a thousand other studies. They fully answer this objection.

Then there's the *self-feeding loop* I discovered while writing this book. See chapter six for this diagram:

It would seem that LRT could gradually become a Single Tax and even be able to provide an ample Citizen's Dividend.

Objection: ***"LRT is no panacea."***
Reply: Correct. There are no panaceas.

xxxxxxxxxxxxxxxxxxxxxxxxxxxxxxxxxxxxxxxxxxxxxxxxxxxxxxxxxxxx

Politics

Question: *"Are you a Republican or Democrat, liberal or conservative?"*

Reply: Whatever. I am first and foremost a land taxer. Any of those groups could fit LRT into their principles."

Objection: *"I can't pass judgment on LRT. I'm not a tax expert."*

Reply: That's a copout. Whenever it's been tried, it has produced jobs and prosperity – what else do you need to know? Either you advocate the taxation of land or the taxation of production; if you tax land you create jobs and prosperity, if you tax production you create poverty. It's a decision you can't avoid by claiming ignorance.

Objection: *"Some property owners will pay more tax if we adopt two-rate."*

Reply: Some will - a minority - so LRT should be *gradually* introduced to make the transition easier for them. The few pay-more property owners will enjoy the better society occasioned by LRT.

This minority is likely to be made up largely of absentee landowners and some owners of income-producing property who will have an income flow that will make it easier for them to pay their increase.

If we don't tax land values, we'll have to tax wages, buildings, and other human-produced goods and services. That's neither just nor prosperity-inducing.

Objection: *"LRT will hurt retailers. They'll pay more in taxes."*

Reply: Not so, for these reasons:
(1) If the retailers don't own land (and most of them don't), they'll be down-taxed because there'll be less building tax passed on to them.
(2) If the economy prospers, so will they.
(3) Most of their customers will have more income because they will be taxed less.
(4) The retailers will be able to improve their stores without tax penalty.

__Objection:__ "We can't bring in LRT until most voters support it."
__Reply:__ So educate them: are you doing your part? If they're informed about LRT, they'll like it, if only because it will reduce taxes on what they produce.

__Objection:__ "We already have too much development in our town. We want to keep it clean and green. Land value taxation would cause land sites to be more fully developed."
__Reply:__ Zone out unwanted development. If you force your town to be clean and green by down-taxing land-sites and making them expensive, then you will force your countryside to be populated. Rather than live in an expensive urban slum, people will move to your suburbs or countryside. They got to live somewhere.

__Objection:__ "Won't LRT adversely affect zoning?"
__Reply:__ No. Land speculators make money by breaking the zoning code and making land-speculation profits; LRT removes the profits from doing that. Bye-bye spot re-zoning. LRT is the friend of zoning.

__Objection:__ "Won't land value taxation increase the tax burden on our historic and aesthetic buildings?"
__Reply:__ No. Such buildings should be zoned tax-free, now or under LRT. If zoned properly, the White House would be safe.

__Objection:__ "Parks, parks. We won't have any parks with LRT."
__Reply:__ A properly located park will increase surrounding land values more than was lost by creating the park. In fact, LRT gives us a way to test a park's effectiveness: if the park increases nearby land values more than its land values, then it was needed.

__Objection:__ "Land by itself has no rental income, so it should not be taxed. But buildings generate an income, so they should be taxed."
__Reply:__ No – land has an imputed annual income (that's what gives it sale value) so it should be taxed. Why penalize buildings by taxing them? In any case, building owners pass on a building tax to their generally poorer tenants as higher space-rent.

Objection: *"There are many elderly property owners in our town; won't they pay more property tax with LRT?"*

Reply: Probably not. Compared to the average property in town, the elderly have a greater-than-average percentage of their investment in their building (which will be down-taxed) rather than in their land, so they'll pay less if the building tax is transferred to a land tax. Many empirical studies support this. Be kind to your elderly – up-tax land, down-tax their buildings.

In any case, we could exempt the elderly or allow them to defer the LRT until the time of sale or bequest of the land, or we can defer any increase that the tax shift from buildings to land might cause them.

Objection: *"We've already shifted some taxes off buildings onto land value. The results were good. What more can we do?"*

Reply: Do it again. Since it worked well once, shift some more. Don't stop now.

Objection: *"How should the various levels of government – national, state, local – divide the land-rent revenue?"*

Reply: Any way that's convenient. I would suggest 40% for the national government, 25% for state and 35% for local – this reflects the current tax distribution but it is not writ in stone.

Objection: *"You're over-simplifying."*

Reply: If you think so, present logic and facts.

Objection: *"It seems like an exaggeration to say that in the long run, LRT is necessary to preserve free enterprise and democracy."*

Reply: If LRT can end poverty and unemployment, as the hard evidence indicates, if it can lessen depressions/recession and inflation, etc., then it is no exaggeration to say that in the long run LRT is necessary to preserve free enterprise and democracy. If society's basic relationship to nature is wrong, freedom and prosperity won't long survive.

Objection: "The 2-rate property tax is a good idea, but it requires a major change."

Reply: Not if done gradually. All most localities need do is specify different tax rates for building assessments and land assessment in their usual end-of-year property-tax ordnance (instead of their usual one rate for both). States and federal governments can also gradually substitute LRT for other taxes. Governmental revenue will remain constant.

If a federal land value tax replaced the highly regressive 7.65% payroll tax in whole or in part, most people would get tax reductions; *every* wage earner would get a take-home pay increase.

Objection: "You say 2-rate will give most people tax reductions, it can be revenue-neutral for the government, and there'll be a spurt in new construction and renovation. That's too good to be true! You can't get blood out of a turnip."

Reply: What you say about turnips is true enough, but these land-taxing benefits have occurred *in actual practice*. Scores of empirical studies are in full substantiation. If you think it's too good to be true, present evidence.

Objection: "Whoa! We can't get something for nothing."

Reply: Definitely. But LRT ensures the proper use of land while providing revenue for the government. What's wrong with that?

Objection: "The Single Tax won't sell. Only sex sells, and there's no sex in it."

Reply: Yes there is: SinglE taX.

Objection: "What's the difference what is taxed? It all comes out of income."

Reply: Some taxes are better than others. Don't tax what you produce, tax land instead. Land tax good, all other taxes bad (for you and for the economy).

Objection: *"I don't believe in evidence when it comes to distant economic theories. I believe what I believe. Don't confuse me with the facts. It's a free country. I'll always believe LRT is too good to be true. Besides, it's revolutionary and won't change anything."*

Reply: No doubt about it - you certainly believe what you believe (but is what you believe – true?).

xxxxxxxxxxxxxxxxxxxxxxxxxxxxxxxxxxxxxxxxxxxxxxxxxxxxxxx

Summation

LRT	OTHER TAXES
(1) increases incentive to use sites fully	(1) decreases incentive to produce
(2) neither increases price or rents	(2) adds to both prices and rents
(3) cannot be evaded or avoided	(3) subject to evasion and avoidance
(4) based on what the community provides	(4) private property confiscated (as on wages and purchases)
(5) reasonably precise	5) requires thousand of pages of rules
(6) cheap to collect	(6) requires great clerical costs for govt. and taxpayers (think audit-phobia)

The trouble with taxing rich guys is that there aren't enough of them to support the rest of us in the style to which we would like to become accustomed.

xxxxxxxxxxxxxxxxxxxxxxxxxxxxxxxxxxxxxxxxxxxxxxxxxxxxxxx

Addendum

<u>***Objection:*** *"I can't decide. I'm not an expert."*</u>

Reply: (1) Copout. What is there about the ethics or substantiation offered in this book that you can't decide about?

(2) On what basis do you choose an expert to decide for you?

(3) If buildings and other produced things are down-taxed, won't we have more and better buildings and produced things? What can't you understand about that? If land is up-taxed, wouldn't that require land under-users to develop their sites? You can't decide about that?

XXXXXXXXXXXXXXXXXXXXXXXXXXXXXXXXXXXXXXXXXXXXXXXXXXXXXXXX
XXXXXXXXXXXXXXXXXXXXXXXXXXXXXXXXXXXXXXXXXXXXXXXXXXXXXXXX

+

> *The Center for the Study of Economics (1518 Walnut St. [#604], Philadelphia, Pa. 19102 (ph. 215-545-6004, fax 215-545-4929, incentivetaxation@urban tools.net) has a handsome booklet entitled "44 Objections & Responses" - send $5 (as of 2005) for it.*

9

If land value taxation is as good as the logic and facts indicate, it is perfectly legitimate to ask why it hasn't been more widely adopted. Twenty-two reasons are given.

Again, the format is different.

Chapter **9**

Why Not Widely Adopted

If the proposal is as good as it seems, if it is ethically demanded and has so much empirical support, it is natural to ask why it has not been more widely adopted. After all, free enterprise and democracy are constantly being whittled away by ever-increasing taxes and repressive laws to which only LRT is the long-run antidote. Why isn't it being more widely adopted now?

Listed here are 22 reasons why LRT has not been more widely adopted.

(1) *Land is thought to be no different than any other commodity* so many think it shouldn't be singled out for taxation. In fact, they actually feel sorry for the owners of vacant land because they have no current income from it.

Not so long ago, land was commonly regarded as the ultimate source of all wealth and therefore different than human-produced wealth. It no longer is so regarded. Now people think of it as just another commodity like any other.

Once, landowning was identified with the distrusted, non-working, arrogant nobility who got their land from the government or from a king who were regarded as the ultimate landowners. Today, the government as the ultimate landowner has become a mere legal fiction, justifying nothing more than eminent domain.

(2) *The LRT aficionados are not concerned with finding out how to implement LRT <u>in the foreseeable future</u>.* They abhor the compromises of politics. They primarily focus on the wonderful Single Tax theory. They seek to tax land values all at once everywhere, but that doesn't sell politically.

They go to sleep dreaming of the Single Tax but they don't inquire how to do it in the foreseeable future. Also, they talk about making land common property, but that turns people off.

They show no interest in the simple formulas I have offered them for implementing the land rent tax in the foreseeable future (I have about 45), but fortunately there has been one outstanding exception – my former executive assistant who is now winning some LRT victories of his own. You, dear reader, can easily learn how to implement LRT and save rational civilization (see the appendix).

(3) *The identification of LRT with Henry George has been counter-productive.* Many critics discard not only George's arguments for LRT, but all of LRT as well. His identification of widespread poverty as *an inevitable concomitant* of non-LRT progress is contrary to the obvious facts. In addition, many critics discard LRT because they feel that it cannot be a Single Tax.

(4) *The implementation of LRT in the foreseeable future has to be so gradual that its benefits aren't noticed.* The small first steps to enact it provide hard-to-notice benefits. Building-permit increases excite few people; LRT is often thought to be OK but of limited value, or it is disregarded altogether even though its critics don't provide hard factual data.

(5) ***The opponents of LRT often make big political contributions*** while the Georgists stay at home and grumble (thinking "you can't fight City Hall").

These opponents are apt to have large landholdings and are especially likely to be connected to the car culture. In the past, auto dealers, gas stations, parking lots, convenience stores, fast-food outlets, etc. have been vocal opponents, though their anti-LVT influence will be less felt on the state or national scene.

For example, consider auto dealers. They under-utilize vast urban lots on which they park cars for sale, which means they generally would pay more with LRT, and this drives them into opposition to LRT; they still do business in town but they should now be located just outside of town where land is cheaper. They exercise a strong anti-LRT influence on their local newspapers because of their extensive newspaper advertising.

(6) ***Many untutored laymen think you can't separate land values from building values.*** They tend to merge land value into building value and therefore regard a land value tax as being a tax on the house they live in, even though most homeowners and all tenants would save money with LRT. But they're simply unaware of that.

(7) ***The property tax is not particularly popular because it comes as one inconvenient budget-busting annual charge.*** As it happens, LRT is a type of property tax and so is tarred with the same brush as is the property tax. Yet most people would save if LRT replaced other taxes and there are many ways to prevent this big disliked one-time payment.

For instance, the property tax could be paid on the same withholding basis that has made the burdensome income tax bearable (this withholding provision was first developed by Milton Friedman, of all people, during World War II).

It's worth noting here that in the first century of American history, the property tax was the chief support of government (the tariff was the preferred tax at the national level).

(8) ***Few people know about LRT, so they distrust it.*** They think it stands little chance of being adopted and are unaware that hundreds of cities worldwide have used it. That even is true of most tax professionals.

It is said that nothing succeeds like success. True, but nothing fails like failure.

In today's economy of ours, taxing land values doesn't seem important – even though the more we tax human-produced goods and services, the lower goes the price of land and the more it seems economically unimportant. A self-fulfilling prophecy!

Many people just can't believe there's a tax than can promote the economy and create jobs. You can show them the facts, but it's like water off a duck's back. They expect to suffer from taxes.

"Land tax good, all other taxes bad" – their reaction is "huh?"

(9) *Republicans and conservatives reflexively oppose _all_ taxes, even land taxes.* The result is that they fight hard for small tax decreases while the tax level constantly escalates over the decades. They can't seem to realize they're fighting a losing battle that can only be won by the adoption of LRT.

Liberals will tax anything (even land) but they tend to be more interested in subsidizing poverty.

(10) *Politicians fail to stress that LRT will give most people tax reductions.* Wouldn't the voters favor LRT if they were aware they'd get tax reductions? "Vote Yourself a Tax Break" could be a compelling political slogan.

It is vitally important to *continually* inform the voters of the tax break most of them could qualify for. One good way for localities to so inform them is to enclose a description of LRT along with the property-tax notice that is sent annually to property taxpayers.

It may be hard to get the LRT Bandwagon rolling, but once it starts to roll, it will be hard to stop. Politicians will then be either in the driver's seat or left behind.

(11) *Many people today insist on factual evidence in their daily and business lives, but on political and economic issues they are satisfied with preconceived notions,* which is why they can disregard the vast amount of factual evidence for LRT.

Americans today increasingly embrace solipsism ("only I exist" which leads to the view that each person is the ultimate source of ethical standards, at least for public issues, even if hard factual evidence must be brushed aside). Solipsism is held in low philosophical repute but is nevertheless widely practiced.

(12) *The land tax __rate__ is apt to be so high* as to cause many taxpayers to unthinkingly oppose LRT. This is apt to be particularly true at the local level.

(13) *Many people think taxation should be based on ability-to-pay* so they tend to oppose LRT, not realizing that it is the most ability-to-pay major tax there is. The enthusiasts for taxing rich guys are really penalizing the efficient to subsidize poverty via government welfare expenditures (with the average guy footing the tax bill).

(14) *The rise of governmentalism* – many people increasingly look to government handouts for solving social problems.

(15) *The rise of ethical relativism,* which maintains that ethical principles are not rationally provable (but since ethical relativism is itself an ethical principle, it is by its own terms unprovable!). The ethical arguments advanced for the taxation of land values strike no responsive chord with many people. They seem to prefer "plucking the goose with the least squawk" (but it's the average taxpayer who ends up squawking).

(16) *The rise of anti-growth sentiment.* Many people nowadays want jobs and wealth, but they don't want development in their own neighborhood. This is often known as NIMBY-ism, but now many have gone BANANAs – Build Absolutely Nothing Anywhere Near Anybody. Where then? (maybe on clouds). They should be advised that jobs and wealth don't grow on trees.

Because LVT promotes growth, it seems opposed to environmentalism.

(17) *LRT is not supported by an identifiable political constituency.* Many people are uncomfortable with new ideas.

(18) *"It sounds too good to be true."* Ask those who raise this objection to present evidence.

(19) *Many people accept land speculation because they imagine that some day they might win at that game (i.e., they hope to get something for nothing) and they take vicarious pleasure in those few that do win.* But at least the many people who lost money on sweepstake tickets voluntarily bought them and others aren't asked to pay for their addiction.

(20) *Currently, there are only two organizations that have induced any land rent taxation in the U.S.* They are the Henry George Foundation of America and the Center for the Study of Economics (1518 Walnut St., #604, Philadelphia, Pa. 19102, 1-215-545-6004); they work together. Unfortunately, each one is poorer than the other (so to speak). They are on the financial knife's edge and very much need contributions from the many who would benefit from what they do.

(21) *The untutored voters are apt to viscerally oppose LRT,* thinking they'd pay more in taxes, which of course is generally not so.

Also, many voters don't want to think about taxes. They oppose them all, the good and the bad alike. If politicians were to implement a little LRT gradually and give the voters actual tax reductions, they would easily get re-elected and we'd have some LRT.

But frankly, it's not only the voters who are untutored but many federal officials as well. They just assume without any constitutional basis whatsoever that the federal government can't tax land rent, that it's a local or state function only. So they tax tax tax the producers of wealth.

(22) *A land assessment is required.* This is not difficult but it does take time, commitment and patience, qualities often in short supply. Just about every community in America already assesses land values (an advantage America has over many other countries). The assessments are sometimes inaccurate, but that is correctable. State and federal governments can make use of these assessments right away to institute LRT.

(23) *It is not clear that the prosperity engendered by LRT has been due to LRT,* whereas if a tax break is given to a specific firm to relocate in town, then it is obvious why the town got this new employer.

Despite all this, LRT has nevertheless been rather widely adopted in the world, especially in Australia, New Zealand, western Canada, South Africa, and Denmark, as well as in 22 U.S. localities (as of this writing), but nowhere as a Single Tax.

If you, dear reader, accept LRT but intend to do nothing in its behalf, then maybe you aren't entitled to ask why it has not been more widely adopted.

10

This is a brief concluding chapter (1,116 words) summarizing what has gone before.

It is not advisable to start reading this book with this chapter, as what it maintains will seem too good to be true. It is necessary to first become familiar with the logical arguments and empirical substantiation for the book's main proposal.

chapter **10**

Last Word

Those who read this last chapter first are likely to doubt that land rent taxation can ensure continuous prosperity and the long-run future of free enterprise and democracy. But those who have read the previous chapters have seen the massive empirical evidence showing that it has already accomplished these things. Is it not then the most important idea ever conceived?

Hasn't it been proven both logically and empirically that other reforms are like re-arranging the deck chairs on the *Titanic?* Doesn't the future of civilization literally depend on its adoption?

To the extent that land rent taxation has actually been tried, it has *always* worked. *There are 237 empirical cases supporting it, and there are more!* How much more substantiation do you want?

This is what the logic and empirical evidence presented in this book can promise with LRT:

1) Most voters would get actual tax reductions (because they have little land rent income) with no reduction in government revenue

2) Taxes on human production can be eliminated entirely; imagine how prosperous we could be if all production were tax-free

3) All land sites would be efficiently used and land prices would be reduced (eventually eliminated); wouldn't this result in a huge increase in wealth production?

4) Producers would not have to sink huge sums up-front to buy land in order to produce

5) Depressions and inflations can be minimized

If this book can achieve these five benefits, plus many others, then it can lay claim to proposing an important idea. Is it not the world's last chance?

We have seen how well a little land rent taxation has worked - *imagine what 100% land rent taxation would do!*

Yet there will be disparagers of this reform: "Taxes have always been with us...landowners will suffer...It's all a matter of opinion... We'll have to change our way of doing things...We're doing well enough now (at least I am)... Don't rock the boat..."

"It can't be done...Justice is nice but impractical...Didn't Henry George advocate this...Not right now - let's think about it...etc."

More: "It stands little chance of adoption (so did democracy once)...Few have heard of the proposal (yet)...I want to be on the winning side (you could be)."

If you encounter critics, be sure to ask them to present clear logic and hard hard evidence, not just fulmination.

To claim that free enterprise and democracy depend on land rent taxation – well, we've already briefly discussed this, but in this final chapter let's see what we can add. After all, some pollyannas might still think that land rent taxation is a good idea, but if we don't do it, we'll be all right anyway. No:

(1) Without land rent taxation, future tax increases on production are inevitable. Burgeoning social problems will increasingly demand government action.

(2) These increasing taxes will not only burden our economy but will violate property rights. They will gradually suffocate democracy (maybe even majority rule). We stand in danger of slowly taxing ourselves into socialism and "benevolent" dictatorship.

(3) This book has shown that land rent taxation could replace not only all other taxes but could even provide a generous Citizen's Dividend (think how that would inundate poverty!). To readers who start with this last chapter, this will seem to be a gross exaggeration.

In order to tax land rent, we have to start out taxing the selling price of land, but we should switch as soon as possible to taxing land rent directly; it is the basis for the land's selling price.

Like all taxes, the tax on land rent collects governmental revenue, but in every other way it is exactly the opposite of all the other taxes. There's a section in chapter one which discusses this at length. We have seen how land rent taxation can help farmers, promote the environment, and even combat terrorism.

For the past thirty years, I have labored hard to get land rent taxation adopted. I was able to get 18 cities and 2 special districts to shift some of their property tax off buildings onto land, with measurable success in every researched case. But it was like dropping a stone in water with no ripples resulting. Despite all my studies (they were publicized) there simply wasn't any popular resonance. Alas, it was no easier when I retired than when I began.

Even today, I ask people, "If we tax buildings less, won't we have more buildings? Will the earth shrink if it is taxed?" I get the obvious answers, but still no resonance. It's still uphill work to spread the idea...but maybe the tide will turn. We don't have much time left.

I have, of course, thought of giving up and joining the herd, but how can I? Heaven on earth beckons; disaster awaits if nothing is done. Well, maybe if you've come this far in the book, you, dear reader, will do something...

Conservatives: we can noodle around with occasional small production-tax cuts here and there, but without land rent taxation, the tax burden on the real producers has risen steadily and will continue to do so because the voters have become willing to pay taxes on what they produce in order to get government services. We endanger free enterprise and democracy if we fail to tax land rent.

Liberals: taxes on things produced end up being paid by the poor. Their income is cut, the prices they pay are boosted, their job opportunities are reduced. Yet they are the very people we should be helping the most. I thank you for providing whatever support in the past that I have been able to achieve.

Upon re-reading this final chapter, I notice that I discussed the empirical evidence for land rent taxation rather fully but only lightly touched upon the impeccable ethical arguments for it. Sorry about that; see chapter two. Our land and tax systems cannot long violate rationality with impunity. Be sure to discard ethical arguments that can also justify slavery, monopoly or thievery. Then if it's right, do it.

Be sure the critics cite hard statistical facts for their point of view. They can't; we'll win, 237-0. What, they're going to try to show that when land is taxed, it won't be used more efficiently and increase GDP? They might as well attempt to attack the Law of Averages...

If our relation to Nature is wrong, democracy will pass into history's dustbin. We can choose either up or down, not sideways. We haven't seen the end of history yet.

Dear reader, your time for decision has come. *Who have you spoken to today about land rent taxation?* Let's end the regular part of this book with these three now fully substantiated conclusions:
Land tax good, all other taxes bad
Tax the value of locations, not things produced
Save free enterprise & democracy
*

Appendix

This book has fully proven both ethically and empirically that land rent should be taxed in preference to the taxation of labor & capital (at first, this requires the taxation of land values).

It is now incumbent upon us to determine how exactly to implement this tax, be it federal, state or local, in the foreseeable future.

Two ethical matters are also listed herein, as well as an extra 50 empirical studies.

Appendix

The chief obstacle to the adoption of LVT in the United States has been knowing how to implement it *in the foreseeable future*. Few Americans know how to do it. Now you can learn. Fortunately, it isn't difficult.

These suggestions were devised mainly with U.S. conditions in mind, but they could obviously apply to any nation.

In addition, some other matters are considered.

A. Land-Valuing Techniques

Let's start by dispelling the neophyte's myth that land assessing is guesswork. Many good books have been written about land assessing and there are many professional courses dealing with it. Highly detailed maps listing land values per front foot can make land assessments accurate. Here is a list of fourteen land assessing techniques (there are many more):

1. Compare the land site we are assessing to the arms-length sale of similarly located vacant land-sites. Accurate sales-price information is a necessity, but that has not been a major problem; for falsifying such information, the law imposes severe penalties, such as disbarment and jail for lawyers and jail for the buyers and sellers (there are too many people involved for falsification).

2. If land is leased, the lease determines the land assessment.

3. There is a definite relationship between the sale price of land and its annual rent: sale price = annual lease-amount divided by the current real-estate interest rate. Thus, if the land-site is leased for $10,000 a year and the current real-estate interest rate is 10%, then the sale price is $100,000.

4. If a building is demolished after an arms-length sale, then this informs us as to the land assessment: it is likely to be the sale price

of the total property plus whatever the purchaser pays for the cost of demolition.

5. If properties with similar buildings are priced differently, the difference is due to the higher land value of the higher-priced property.

6. We can use the capitalized income approach for assessing land value: it is the expected net income of the entire property minus the building income (knowable if the building has been constructed recently and is appropriate to the site).

7. If the building is properly located, we can arrive at the land value by subtracting its value from the total price of the property (land and building) and comparing it to similar land sites. The value of such a building is its replacement cost as determined by the many available construction manuals (taking into account inflation and depreciation).

If the building is not properly located (although it may once have been) then the entire price of the property plus the costs of demolition and construction is to be ascribed to the land value. For example, if a bowling alley on a busy thoroughfare is no longer the site's highest-and-best use and cannot be adequately renovated, then the selling price of the building is zero and the entire value of the property plus demolition cost is land value.

8. If a recently built properly located building is selling for a higher price than its construction cost, then the extra price is probably land value.

9. Often the land value is customarily a certain fraction (say, a third) of the total value of a certain type of a land-and-building parcel. Recent sales of similarly situated properties can ascertain that value.

10. Similar streets, neighborhoods and even cities should have the same land assessment (i.e., locational value).

11. Fire insurance companies are accurately assessing building values (but not the underlying land because it doesn't burn). Assessors can make use of such assessments.

12. Farmland can be assessed based on soil type.

13. Assessments could be phased in over a period of three years or so, with inflation adjustments based on the C.P.I. until the next re-assessment can take place.

14. The work of assessors would be easier if only land need be assessed; that's obviously simpler than assessing both land and buildings.

There are still other land assessment techniques. Good land assessing may be an art as well as a science, but it's not guesswork.

The law should specify the methods to be used, keeping in mind that perfection can be the enemy of the good-enough.

Assessors have often let their land assessments slip below the actual market value of land. To guard against this, local, state and federal authorities should be empowered to challenge land assessments in court if the suit is successful, the assessor's office could be charged for all court costs. We already have state equalization boards to perform this task.

B. Alleviations

Here are eleven ways to alleviate those who are hardshipped by LRT (or even by the current property tax):

1. Defer all or part of the tax to the time of sale or inheritance for the elderly, low-income, and temporarily unemployed. This deferral could apply to either the whole amount of the property tax, or just to the property tax on buildings, or even only to those cases resulting in an increased tax resulting from the introduction of LRT.

2. Provide a cap or limit of 2% plus the inflation rate on property-tax increases due to increased rates.

For example, if the inflation rate has been 2½%/yr. for the past year, a property owner paying $10,000 in property tax in the past year need pay no more than $10,450 in the next year ($10,000 + $10,000 x [.02 + .025]. If the inflation rate is 3% in the second year, then the property owner need pay no more in the second year than $10,972.50 ($10,450 + [$10,450 x [.02 + .03]), assuming no re-assessment.

The inflation rate could be the official BLS estimate for the previous year as usually announced in February, or it could be the ten-month estimate for the previous year, announced earlier than February.

We can assume that property owners can well afford an annual 2% real increase in property-tax liability.

3. Provide withholding for the LRT (even for the current property tax). If the mortgage holder does not make the payment, it could be payable quarterly by the employer (*à la* the income tax) so that the property-tax bill doesn't arrive once a year in an undesirable lump sum.

4. Other taxes can pay the extra property tax of those who pay more with LRT (or perhaps just for the elderly, poor or temporarily unemployed). This is already done in some states for the current property tax and is called a "circuit-breaker."

5. Provide a government loan fund to pay the property tax of those who are hardshipped by the property-tax change (or just for the elderly, poor, or temporarily unemployed).

6. Provide a land value tax rebate – a land-tax payment receipt can be used to obtain a 50% or 100% rebate on other local taxes, or such receipts can be used only by farmers, homeowners, the poor, temporarily unemployed.

7. Provide a purchase-and-demolition (P.A.D.) reimbursement – The local government could reimburse a building owner for the appraised value of his improvement if it is demolished and replaced within a year (in order to prevent circumvention of the law, the old building must be at least 12 years old and its replacement must be of greater appraised value).

This is more protection than building owners have now from an unexpected veering of urban development in their direction. This protection would be less needed if the LRT introduction were gradual.

8. Provide building-assessment abatements (perhaps $500 or so) for such special groups as farmers, homeowners, the elderly, poor, or temporarily unemployed. Or perhaps a percentage of the building assessment could be abated.

9. Provide building-tax exemptions for the above-mentioned special groups. This could also be done for an ordinary property tax.

10. Exempt the first $1,000 of the land tax. In particular, this would help the poor, elderly or temporarily unemployed. The

land tax rate would have to be somewhat higher to replace the lost revenue.

11. Establish a Property-Tax Alleviation Board – This board (either national, state or local) could provide pre-determined hardship reductions in the property tax.

Keep in mind that the *gradual* implementation of LRT is itself a type of alleviation; it gives landowners time to adjust. Experience shows that under LRT only a small minority will pay more (generally slightly) and they tend to be absentee landowners who are hurting the local business climate.

The voters are likely to support a land-tax rate increase if the extra revenue is spent on popular projects, like parks, playgrounds, and highways. Alternative taxes will be more onerous.

I can highly recommend a pamphlet (full disclosure: I wrote it myself) published by the Center for the Study of Economics, 1518 Walnut St., Philadelphia, Pa. 19102, 1-215-545-6004, entitled "14 Alleviations of Special-Case Hardships to Accompany the Government Collection of the Land Rent in Place of Taxes on Producers" (cost $5 as of 2005). Not only Americans can make use of it.

C. How The Federal Government Can Institute a Land Value Tax

Start by reading "Legal Suggestions for Enacting Land Value Taxation" (I happen to be the author). It contains 43 specific suggestions and is published by the Lincoln Institute of Land Policy, 113 Brattle St., Cambridge MA 02138-3400, 1-800-LAND-USE.

In America, there are two constitutional bases for a federal LRT:

1) Article 1, Section 2 of the Constitution says that Congress can apportion direct taxes to the states according to their proportion of the U.S. population. Thus, if a state has 5% of the U.S. population, it must pay 5% of a direct tax specified by the federal government.

A direct tax is a tax that can't be passed on to others in a higher price. There are only three direct taxes - the poll tax, the income tax, and the LRT. Congress taxed land values in 1798, 1813, 1815, and 1861.

2) The 16th Amendment also clearly authorizes Congress to levy an LRT. Here is its exact wording in full: "The Congress shall have power to lay and collect taxes on incomes, *from whatever source derived,* without apportionment among the several States, and without regard to any census or enumeration" (italics added for emphasis). LRT is clearly an income "from whatever source derived."

So there is no constitutional impediment whatever to a federal land value tax. I personally prefer the income-tax approach of the 16th Amendment because that's what Congress and the voters are accustomed to.

If the income tax rate on wages and capital investment is somewhat reduced and the revenue loss made up by a federal land value tax, the economy would benefit and most voters would get a tax reduction (because a significant portion of their income doesn't come from land rent).

Or you might prefer that we replace, in whole or in part, the highly regressive payroll tax (6.2% for Social Security or 7.65% for S.S. and Medicare) with an ability-to-pay good-for-the-economy tax like a federal LRT. Then *every* wage earner would get an immediate take-home pay increase, most voters would get tax reductions, the economy would boom, and the federal government would lose no revenue at all.

The transition costs of social security privatization would then be paid for not by a tax on production but on land rent.

Also, cities and states could replace the federal payroll tax of their residents (in whole or in part) with a land value surtax.

But an LRT requires a land assessment. Fortunately, that's not a major problem because just about every parcel of land in America is assessed locally. The federal government can use these assessments, but it must prevent local assessors from favoring their voters and neighbors by under-assessing land.

The federal government can do this by generously paying the local assessors for their provision of the assessment data (a payment to which the local assessors are clearly entitled) but the payment should be reduced according to the following schedule:

If the current ratio of taxable land assessments to recent market sales is-	then the federal payment will be reduced as follows:
100% or more	0%
99%	0%
98.00%	0%
97.00%	10%
96.00%	30%
95.00%	50%
90.00% or less	100%

The federal government could be granted the option of reassessing the land in particular localities if it feels the land assessments are inaccurate. The reassessments could be offered to the localities at cost. If there are land parcels that aren't assessed (rare), a few federal assessors would be needed to assess them; these assessments could also be sold to the affected localities.

Some states have a composite assessment only (i.e., land and building assessments combined into one assessment) in contradiction to IAAO principles and almost every assessment manual. For federal tax purposes, it can be assumed that in those states the land assessment is 40% of the total composite assessment.

If the federal government wants to introduce 100% LRT, it should do so *gradually,* perhaps 10% of the land rent could be taxed in the first year (to replace other taxes, of course); in the second year, perhaps 20% more land rent could be taxed, then 30% more in the third year, and finally 40% more thereafter. Other percentages are possible.

The federal government can increase the LRT's progressivity by spending most of the revenue obtained in the poorer states.

D. Fourteen Additional Suggestions for a Federal LRT

1. Establish a Federal Assessment Board with the responsibility to assess the land-rental value throughout the country. These assessments could be made available to localities for a fee. The states could then dispense with their own costly assessment equalization boards, nor would the localities need an assessment office.

Or maybe a Federal Equalization Board can be established to oversee local assessment uniformity throughout the U.S. This would cost less than all the current state equalization boards.

2. Land Gains Tax – To determine the taxable land value both when the land was originally purchased and when it is sold, subtract the land assessment (market value) when the property was bought from the market land assessment when it was sold; if a state doesn't distinguish between land and building assessments, then for the purposes of this federal tax, land assessments can be assumed to be 40% of the total property assessment. This could get rid of the anti-economy capital-gains tax.

3. For Specific Expenses - The revenue from a federal land tax could be used to pay (in whole or in part) for a specific expense, such as for social security privatization, payroll taxes, deficit payments, etc.

4. Reform the Income Tax by Setting a Higher Rate on Land Rent Income (Than on Wages or Capital-Interest Income - This should be done by gradually raising the income-tax rate on land income – be it collected or imputed - and correspondingly lowering the rate on wages and capital-interest.

Imputed income is federally taxable, as when Congress taxes estimated waiter's tips (even though not declared), valuable corporate-parking spaces, subsidized company-cafeteria meals and day-care facilities, zero-coupon bond interest figured prior to due date, etc. If you lend money to yourself at less than the applicable federal rate (called AFR), the IRS will impute the difference to you as income and tax you for it.

The IRS can tax the imputed income of land-rent (such as when the same owner owns a land-site and the building on it) by multiplying the assessed land value by the AFR. If the land was owned by one person but rented to someone else (as with a leasehold arrangement) there's no doubt that the land rent would then be taxed.

5. A Federally Funded New City – H.U.D. could offer land to a new city provided: (a) the new city will rent out (not sell) all building-sites to private developers and home buyers, (b) the annual revenue so obtained would replace all local taxes on production, (c) public expenditures would be limited to the inflation rate plus 2%,

(d) surpluses are to go to H.U.D. as reimbursement. States could also do this.

The city would be immediately free of all local taxes. It would provide a clear demonstration of LRT's efficacy. Neither developers nor homebuyers would have to buy land and H.U.D.'s eventual cost would be zero; it might even make a profit.

Such a city could be called Elysium, Illyria, Eldorado or Georgetown, or the first 1,000 residents could be given the right to choose the name of the new city.

6. Exempt Local Land Taxes (not Building Taxes) from the Federal Income Tax, either in whole or in part. If this were done, local assessors would be motivated to assess land closer to market value than buildings.

7. Corporate Income-Tax Investment Deduction – Allow corporations to deduct the full cost of capital investment, but not for land, from their taxable corporate income. This would encourage much-needed capital investment.

8. Federal LRT Enterprise Zones – The federal government now funds enterprise zones in various cities throughout the country and specifies that LRT must be used therein. Or it could tax all future increases in annual land rent in those zones. That would ensure enterprise zone success.

9. Federal Grant Preferences for LRT – H.U.D. and D.O.T. make grants to localities for various purposes and attach qualifications to these grants; shouldn't they give preference to localities that are setting a higher tax rate on land than on buildings? These localities should be rewarded for helping themselves; other localities could do likewise.

Localities could have their federal grants enhanced by 20% for every one percent (or fraction thereof) by which their land tax rate exceeds their building tax rate as figured on full market-value assessment (but no locality could get more than triple its previous years' grant).

For example, if a locality taxes land assessments at 2.3% and buildings at 1.7% on a 60% assessment-to-market ratio, then its federal grant can be enhanced by 7.2% ([2.3% - 1.7%] x 60% x 20%). Other grant formulas are possible.

Another approach: a minimum LRT could be required to qualify for a federal grant. The federal government could legitimately impose such requirements because its grants for sewers, water, roads, airports, flood control, irrigation, etc. enhance local land values.

10. <u>Lease Federally-Owned Lands</u> – The federal government owns almost one-third of the U.S. land area; cities and states own still more. Some of that land should be rented to private individuals subject to annual lease re-assessment with leaseholders' option to renew and right of court appeal. Only federal agency action would be required, no new laws. This would bring in extra revenue.

11. <u>Bond Purchase Plan</u> – The government (federal, state or local) could issue bonds to buy available land-sites at their assessed market value from those wishing to sell. These land users would then pay an annual rent for their sites and could use them as they wish (subject to zoning laws).

The government would incur no net cost because the land rent collected by the government would pay the bond interest; land-sites would then have to be used efficiently (thereby multiplying job opportunities). When the land-purchase bonds will be fully paid off, taxes on payrolls, incomes, sales, businesses, buildings, etc. could be replaced (further enhancing land-rents).

12. <u>Federal LRT Assessment Grants</u> – H.U.D. could make grants to states and cities for improving assessment accuracy and re-assessment frequency.

13. <u>U.S. Foreign Aid for LRT</u> - when U.S. A.I.D. (Agency for International Development) gives money to less-developed countries to build roads, wells, irrigation networks, etc., it should specify that the affected land should be fully taxed; otherwise, local landowners would reap windfall profits and the third-world poor will be little benefited; the World Bank and I.M.F. should do this also. In addition, these agencies should fund land-rent assessments in recipient countries.

14. <u>Federal LRT Research</u> – H.U.D. could fund or publicize empirical studies on LRT. It wouldn't cost much.

Readers are invited to add to this list. Clearly, there's no shortage of ways to implement LRT. Where there's a will, there's a way.

E. Determining Who Pays More, Who Less

Wherever possible, do a who-pays-more-who-less study *before* seeing your LRT prospects. Such a study can easily be done. It is almost sure to demonstrate that most voters will pay less because they don't own much land rent, especially the low-income, elderly and temporarily unemployed. Politicians need not take a leap-in-the-dark.

A quick random survey of the local assessment register is all that is needed to determine this. Those property owners whose own building-to-land assessment ratio is greater than the locality-wide ratio will save with a two-rate LRT-oriented property tax; those with a lower ratio will pay more; those with the same ratio will pay the same.

Only 1% to 5% of the total assessment roll need be random-surveyed. I have found that I can generally survey 120 properties an hour, more if the assessments are on the Internet.

With a computer, you can even more easily survey *every* property, especially in large cities, provided you can obtain the computer disk or tape of the whole assessment roll.

To find out how poor people fare, it will be necessary to consult U.S. census-tract information for any neighborhood, especially poor ones. You can then compare what these people are paying now in property taxes to what they would pay with a building-to-land shift in the property tax. Variations on this approach are possible, such as comparing the median building tax or two-rate payment.

If other taxes, such as on income, sales or payroll, will be transferred to LRT, then compare what the median taxpayer pays in relevant census tracts with what they would pay with LRT (or call C.S.E. at 1-215-545-6004).

U.S. census-tract data is available on the Internet at census.gov.

F. Some Formulas for Implementing A Building-to-Land Tax Shift at the Local Level

The much-maligned local property tax is the worst tax of all, and the best:

Worst – insofar as it falls on much-needed buildings, making them more expensive to construct and operate. Buildings are an absolute necessity to live and work in, so they shouldn't be taxed at all.

Best – insofar as it falls on land, spurring proper land use. If land-sites are under-used, jobs and goods & services are lost.

You can maximize the best of the local property tax and minimize the worst by transferring taxes from buildings to land. I have developed about 45 simple formulas (most are based on the basic property-tax formula, revenue = rate x assessments) and 26 simple procedures for doing this. Here are the two absolutely necessary formulas:

➤ PBTR = 80% x CBTR, where PBTR is the proposed building tax rate and CBTR is the current building one-rate tax. The 80% is not writ in stone. It depends on local attitudes and conditions. It comes from experience; I have found that a smaller percentage would cause a few property owners to get suddenly higher property-tax bills, causing them to go into effective opposition.

If the current property-tax rate is low, then a lower-than-80% figure can safely be used (in America, property-tax rates are apt to be higher than in non-American countries because the local property tax pays for more government services).

➤ PLTR = (CBTR – PBTR) x BA/LA, + CLTR (where PLTR is the proposed land tax rate, CBTR is the current building tax rate, PBTR is the proposed building tax rate arrived at from the above formula, BA is the jurisdiction's total building assessments, LA is the jurisdiction's total land assessments, and CLTR is the current land tax rate). These formulas have the advantage of containing only publicly available data.

There is another mathematically valid formula that can be used instead of the PLTR formula above: PLTR = Revenue - (PBTR x BA)/LA, but I advise against its use because it is often difficult to ascertain revenue accurately (it is not a publicly available figure, it's constantly changing and generally determined at the last minute before adoption of the property-tax rates for the coming year).

Also, budget directors will often give you this year's revenue, whereas this formula requires next year's revenue. So in practice, this formula can have two unknowns (Revenue and PLTR) and cannot be solved.

It is also possible to determine the land tax rate by dividing the revenue lost from the down-taxing of building assessments by the total area-wide land assessment, and then adding that amount to the current land-tax rate.

Remember to suggest specific tax rates on land and buildings to a mayor, budget director, council, board, etc. *before* giving the benefits of LRT.

Reformers must keep their pitch simple. They shouldn't overestimate the LRT knowledge of their prospects. They should use factual arguments primarily. They should be certain beforehand of the jurisdiction's legal requirements. And of course, they should suggest specific land and building tax rates as soon as possible.

Many of the formulas and procedures are listed in about four booklets and are available upon request from C.S.E., 1518 Walnut St. (#604), Philadelphia, Pa. 19102, 215-545-6004 (cost: $5.00 for each booklet, as of 2005).

If LRT is to replace a burdensome non-LRT tax or some new expense, divide them by the total land assessment, or let C.S.E. do the job.

To sum up – unless you know the correct formulas and procedures for implementing LRT, you will have difficulty inducing it in the foreseeable future (but you can always be a cheerleader).

G. Ethical Relativism and Moral Relativism

Ethical relativism asserts that ethical standards can never be proven valid, but since it is itself an ethical standard, by its own admission it can never be proven valid.

By asserting that the equal-rights doctrine is only a personal opinion, it is also socially harmful. A society arguing that way is asking for trouble and will get it. Its enemies also have opinions, generally more strongly held.

Shouldn't religionists be pleased that rationalism supports what they have always preached?

There's a considerable difference between ethics and morals. Ethics concerns itself with ethical *principles* that are rationally provable, whereas morality concerns itself with the actual *applications* of these principles in the real world.

Consider the death penalty, for instance. It involves the taking of a life and that is ethically wrong, but it can be morally justified if it prevents future crimes. Its alternatives are not attractive – they are imprisonment (a form of torture) or fining (a denial of property rights). Moral relativism could be justified in this case. In short, we should be ethical rationalists and moral relativists:

- ❖ Ethical rationalism is always justified (it deals with principles of behavior).
- ❖ Ethical relativism can never be justified.
- ❖ Moral relativism can be justified (since it deals with applications).

Further information about these matters can be found in *Society at the Crossroads.*

H. Herbert Spencer

"Does sale or bequest generate a right where it did not previously exist... No: though nothing be multiplied forever, it will not produce one....

"'But Time,' say some, 'is a great legalizer. Immemorial possession must be taken to constitute a legitimate claim. That which has been bought and sold as such, must now be considered as irrevocably belonging to individuals.' To which proposition a willing assent shall be given when they find satisfactory answers to such questions as, How long does it take for what was originally a wrong to grow into a right? At what rate per annum do invalid claims become valid? If a title gets perfect in a thousand years, how much more than perfect will it be in two thousand years?

"But there are those who will protest, in the beginning, when all land sites were virgin and un-occupied, the first settlers appropriated them one after another. They asserted the right of ownership over these sites just as they might over a lost coin found on the road. The land sites were theirs by right of discovery and priority of occupation; which rights they passed down to their heirs through the generations down to the present time.

"Not quite. Such argument begs the question, for it assumes that the land sites upon which the first settlers stumbled were un-owned to begin with, like the lost coin on the road whose original owner can no longer be traced.

"But this assumption is not valid, since we should all have equal access to the opportunities afforded by nature. Such equal access requires equal ownership of land (since only through ownership can there be access), or more practically, it requires equal ownership of the rent of land.

"Or we can put it another way: to each the fruits of his labor, but since un-taxed land (as distinct from the crop or building on it) is the fruit of no one's labor, then no one can claim exclusive right to it: we all have an equal right to it.

"What the first settlers discovered, then, was something – land sites – which belonged equally to us all, and not exclusively to them. They found something that already belonged to others. Their just claim arising from discovery and settlement was to priority of use that they should continue to enjoy so long as they pay rent to the ultimate owner – society. Of course, at first the rent would be zero but would grow slowly as other people arrived and augmented the demand for the land.

"The proper analogy is between the first settler and the finder of a coin whose owner is clearly known.

"If the origin of all land titles can be traced back to either force or fraud, then the private ownership of land is a privilege which can be justified only by a tax payment to society equal to the value of the privilege." (*Social Statics*, 1850).

I. The Lusht Study

Here is an *empirical* study by Professor Kenneth Lusht, Chairman of the Real Estate Dept. at Penn State University and one of America's leading real-estate economists. It can supplement the 22 empirical studies listed in chapter three and the 50 listed later in this appendix.

Greater Melbourne has many municipalities that are equivalent to neighborhoods in America except that they have the power to tax. Some tax only land value; others nearby don't. Lusht compared the growth rates of these two groups. The Lincoln Institute of Land Policy published his study in 1992.

It was entitled "The Site Value Tax and Residential Development, 1992" (site = land). He sampled 53 of the 56 local government authorities within the Melbourne Statistical District; 29 taxed land sites only and 24 taxed real-estate income. This is his concluding comment:

> *There is evidence that the use of the site value tax stimulates development and that the advantage persists in the long run, though somewhat eroded. The results also suggest that the level of the property tax in Melbourne, which is similar to levels in typical US cities, is sufficiently high to affect behavior. The site value tax was a consistently significant predictor, with most specifications showing 40-60 percent more stock per acre in SV-taxing LGAs [site-value taxing local government authorities].*

Common observation dictates that if you down-tax human-produced things, there will be more of them and they'll be better; if you up-tax land, it will have to be used more efficiently. But it's nice to have a leading scholar offer unimpeachable evidence.

J. Suggested State Laws Enabling Local LRT

1. "Localities authorized to levy a property tax may levy a different percentage rate on land assessments than on building assessments."

2. "Localities authorized to levy a property tax can assess land closer to market value than buildings for tax purposes."

3. "Localities authorized to levy a property tax may exempt building assessments in whole or in part from property taxation."

K. Miscellaneous Ideas

1. Localities should rent out land-sites obtained by tax foreclosures, abandonment, purchase, etc. instead of selling them, subject to triennial renegotiation of the land lease with the new occupant based on current market conditions. The improvements on those sites should be sold outright.

2. 2% of the LRT revenue should be set aside for an advertising campaign for educating the public on what LRT is.

3. Justice Else-Mitchell of Australia proposed to convert titles from freehold to leasehold automatically on the death of the current landholder, or at a period of about fifty years, whichever comes first.

4. Allow a federal tax deduction for state or local LRT (it could raise taxes elsewhere). Most people would get tax reductions and local land assessors would be motivated to assess land more fully. Individual states could decide whether they would take advantage of this federal offer.

5. If a locality has different tax rates for commercial-industrial properties and for residential properties, a two-rate LRT can be instituted for either or both classes.

6. The federal or state governments could provide environmental-protection services (or other land-related services) to a city or county, to be paid for by a surtax on assessed land values.

7. With LRT, only land need be assessed, so re-assessments can easily be annual.

8. Introduce assessment increases by one-third each year for three years.

9. The uniformity clause in most state constitutions is often cited as preventing localities from instituting a two-rate LRT tax. Not so: about two-thirds of the states in the U.S. require only a state legislative enactment to allow localities to tax land and buildings at different rates, even though just about all of them have a uniformity clause.

That clause only requires all land to be taxed uniformly, and all buildings to be taxed uniformly. Land and buildings are different types of property, so different tax rates on land and buildings do not violate the uniformity clause. They needn't be assessed together if the state legislature so wishes.

10. The self-assessment of land is an interesting concept. The landowner assesses his own land parcel, but to prevent under-assessment in order to lower the tax, the government or any individual could buy the land at 10% above the self-assessed price and must then charge a rental to the former owner of no more than 6% of the purchase price.

The government should suggest a proper assessment in order to provide guidance for existing and prospective landowners. Some nations that can't employ experienced assessors might find this approach to be particularly attractive.

11. The revenue from an LRT could be distributed equally to all citizens rather than it being used to eliminate a tax. Such a Citizen's Dividend might be more popular.

12. An LRT payment could be deducted from a landowner's income (like the income tax) instead of arriving once a year in one rather huge payment.

13. Localities could grant complete or partial exemption to all newly constructed buildings (not to the land, of course).

14. Implementation is likely to be different in each country. In the United Kingdom, for instance, national implementation in the foreseeable future by Parliament seems politically difficult. As a first step, local councils should be granted the right to institute a local LRT, as a test case.

15. Leaseholders should have the legal option of buying the improvement on their land at its assessed market value.

L. Fifty More Empirical Studies

This book has two main focuses: the ethical and the empirical. The ethical case is put forth in chapter two and somewhat in this appendix. For the empirical case, see chapter three and has always worked. But there may be some skeptics who need more studies, so here are 50 more:

1. In the early 1970s, the General Council for Rating Reform of Australia reported that in Kilmore Shire, Victoria, the dollar value of

construction and renovation increased 3.19 times in the three whole years after it started to tax land values only, as compared to the three years previous when building and land income were taxed (based on statistics from the Australian Bureau of Census; local property-tax switches in Australia were made in April so there was a year in which both systems applied; see IT, summer 1975).

(2) In Buninyong Shire (Victoria), the GCRR found that, comparing the three whole years immediately prior to the shift from taxing the income of both building and land to the first two whole years after the shift when only the land value was taxed, there was an average 5.9 times increase in the annual dollar value of new construction and renovation (*Ibid.*).

(3) In Orbost Shire (also Victoria), the GCRR compared the three whole years before the land value taxing shift to the year immediately after the shift. It found that average annual construction and renovation increased 1.74 times (*Ibid.*)

(4) Melton Shire (Victoria) switched from taxing real-estate income to taxing only land values in 1973 as the result of a poll of landowners only and then saw the A$ value of its building permits increase 1.68 times in the first year after the switch as compared to the year previous (source: *Ibid.;* see IT 10/75).

(5) The average 1954-61 population growth of rural LRT towns in Victoria was 21.8%, but for their non-LVT neighbors it was only 13.4%. Their 1955-63 dwelling construction was 38.3% higher (source: GCRR, using Victoria state govt. statistics).

(6) New York State taxpayers spent more than $400 million to build the New York Thruway but land values along the route increased by considerably more than $400 million (Perry Prentice, v.p. of Time, Inc. in *Architectural Forum* – IT 1-2/76).

(7) *Life* editorial (1965): "Since the [Toronto] subway was built the neighborhoods around the stations have experienced a small construction boom and land values have skyrocketed. A 100-square-foot plot purchased in 1947 for $22,000 sold ten years later for $257,000." (IT, 1-2/76).

(8) "The landowners on Staten Island in New York City pocketed a $700 million windfall because other taxpayers put up $350 million for the Verrazano Narrows Bridge; now their land is much more

accessible than before. And one can wonder about the increase in land valuation on the Brooklyn side of the bridge." So wrote Perry Prentice in an article in *The Commercial and Financial Chronicle*, 8/22/68 (IT, 1-2/76).

(9) In the seven years following the construction of New York City's IRT subway from 135th St. to Spuyten Duyvil, the rise in land value was $69.3 million. Subtracting the normal increase during the previous seven years - $20.1 million – leaves an increase of $49.2 million directly attributable to the opening of the line. But that section of the line cost only $41.8 million (Gilbert Tucker, *The Self-Supporting City*, quoting a City Club study - see IT, 1-2/76).

(10) According to one public official in New Jersey quoted by Gilbert Tucker in *The Self-Supporting City*, the opening of the George Washington Bridge in 1928 increased land values on just the New Jersey side by $300 million, or more than six times the original construction cost (IT, 1-2/76).

(11) Less than two years after the landowners of Wangaratta (in Victoria, Aus.) had voted 4-1 to adopt LRT only, the local newspaper headlined an article - "Building 'Wave' Envelops Whole of Town." This occurred during a building recession in the general area (IT, 9/75).

(12-27) Random-sample studies in sixteen U.S. cities substantiating that most homeowners pay less with a two-rate building-to-land property-tax shift IT 5-6-7/76).

(28) Two years after adopting an LRT-only property tax, 1957 construction in Mildura City (351 miles northwest of Melbourne) broke all records, "and at the present rate, the 1957 record will be broken this year" (researcher Elizabeth Read Brown in the *Amer. Journal of Economics & Sociology* (1/61, p. 12; see IT 9/76).

(29) "As a means of encouraging owners of sub-standard dwellings to install improvements, the City of New York adopted in 1936 a law granting property-tax exemption for five years upon the value added to existing buildings by improvements completed before October 1, 1938, provided the improvements did not increase the size of the building. Mayor LaGuardia estimated that renovation work in that year ran as high as $75,000,000…" (Harold S. Buttenheim, founding editor of the *American City Magazine* -see IT 11/76).

(30) Then there's Horsham, a city in rural Victoria, Australia). To quote from *Progress,* 6/74 (an Australian monthly magazine): "Horsham made the change to site value rating during the rural recession. For the three years before the un-taxing of buildings, the numbers and values of permits issued to private homebuilders had fallen drastically (from $718,000 down to $418,000 immediately before the change).

"The rot was stopped in the first year of untaxed buildings and the slow climb back commenced. For the year ended 30th June 1973, the numbers of privately built dwelling units approved rose to 94 and their value to $1,153,000.

"This is almost double the numbers of approvals and almost triple their values of the last year of taxed buildings. Site value rating has done much to beat the rural recession in this area." (Australian government building-permit statistics, see IT 12/76).

(31) From 1921 to 1933, 7% of the municipalities in Victoria, Aus. taxed only land values, but they accounted for 46% of home construction. In the years 1947-54, the LRT municipalities had increased to 12%, but they accounted for 42% of the home construction. During 1954-58, 19% were using LRT, but they accounted for 62% of new home construction (building-permit issuance per GCLR). See 1T, 10/77.

(32) Wellington, New Zealand taxed land values while Auckland did not. In 1965, Wellington had £219 in improvements for every £100 in land value while Auckland had only £143 in improvements per £100 in land value (N.Z. govt. statistics per GCLR; see IT, 10/77).

(33) In 1965, LVT-only Sydney had £222 in improvements for every £100 values whereas one-rate Melbourne had only £125 in improvements for every £100 in land values (the two cities are quite comparable; GCLR using the Aus. govt.'s ABS; see IT, 10/77).

(34) Ken Synett (former mayor of Marion, Aus): "For many years the Marion area remained static. Much of the land now being developed was in the hands of speculators.

They held it as a lock-up investment. Tax rates were low...

"Then in 1954, the year after we achieved city status, our rating system was changed from a rental basis [i.e., real-estate-income tax] to one based on unimproved land value. This sent the tax rates up [on land values]…The land investors decided it was time to sell…We are now watching Marion's phenomenal expansion with pride." See IT, 10/77.

(35) After Camberwell, a suburb of Melbourne, Australia, adopted LVT-only in 1922, its development was meteoric. For twenty years, it led in building-development in Victoria in both numbers and values until displaced by Moorabin in 1946 after that city also changed to LRT-only. In addition, Camberwell exhibited another advantage of LRT-only – it was fully in accord with ability-to-pay (*Progress* per LVRG, using Aus. govt. statistics; see chart in IT, 11/77).

(36) A 1965 study sponsored by the California General Assembly and prepared by Griffin, Hagen and Kroger revealed that over 92% of the homeowners and renters in Fresno, CA would get tax reductions with a building-to-land tax shift. See IT 12/77.

(37-41) A GCLR study of five land-taxing towns in rural Victoria, Australia between 1965 and 1966 showed that they exceeded the construction growth of their neighbors by 18%, 23%, 48%, 52% and 66%.

(42) In November 1964, the property owners of South Melbourne (Aus.) voted in a switch to the LRT-only system. In the first six months of 1965, building values increased 2.4 times over what it had been in the four preceding six-month periods. The expenditures for alterations and additions to houses were 2.8 times the average in the four preceding six-month periods. The total value of construction permits for industrial buildings increased 3.3 times.

Not only that, but the growth in construction continued unabated in the ensuing years (Aus. govt. statistics per GCLR).

Many decades ago, South Melbourne had been a fashionable spot in the Melbourne area. Then it ran down, went to seed. After switching to LVT-only, it revived and became known as the "Cinderella City." A headline in the *Melbourne Herald* (12/2/72) called its renaissance "The Kiss of Life" (see IT, 1/78).

(43) The Local Government and Shires Association of Australia reported that "a survey made by the city of Sydney [LRT-only] in 1950, showed that the building taxation system would have penalized

the factory owner, the house investor, the homeowner, and the small shopkeeper, to the benefit of the large business interests in close proximity to the City [downtown]." See IT, 1/78.

(44) H. W. Eastwood (Chief Assessor of New South Wales Province, Aus. in the 1970s) strongly supported local land value taxation, particularly because general re-assessments could be made every two years. His testimony appears in the 1966 Royal Commission of Inquiry into Rating Valuation and Local Government Finance (section 4.25). See IT, 1/78.

(45) Landowners in rural Mildura - pop. 11,000, 350 miles northwest of Melbourne in rural Victoria - voted in LRT-only in August 1956 by a 3.6:1 margin. The value of building permits thereupon rose by one-third in 1957 and by another third in 1958 in the face of a 10% house-building recession in rural Victoria during those years (Aus. govt. statistics as quoted in *Progress* 11/59). See IT, 1/78.

(46) After Moorabin, the largest of the municipalities comprising Greater Melbourne, voted in LRT-only in 1946, its total value of all building permits jumped 21% and within three years they had jumped 141% (Aus. govt. statistics as cited by the *Moorabin Standard-News,* 8/22/58). Especially remarkable was the growth in Cheltenham, which had been a particularly blighted section of Moorabin. See IT, 1/78.

(47) In the country districts of Western Australia, 36 localities taxed land values only; they experienced a 13.34% increase in the total number of dwellings between 6/30/71 and 6/30/76. The 69 localities partly taxing land values only and partly taxing land and buildings together (they use both systems simultaneously) experienced only a 1.53% increase. In other words, the more land was taxed and buildings un-taxed, the more new construction occurred.

It should be noted that the LRT-only localities were distributed rather widely throughout the country districts, also somewhat in the Perth suburbs. They were not concentrated in certain areas where perhaps development proceeded rapidly for special reasons, such as geography, new highways, etc. See IT, Sp/78.

(48) Richard Noyes, when editor of the *Salem (N.H.) Observer,* found that the group in his hometown whose property taxes would

increase the most with a higher tax rate on land was composed of out-of-town land speculators (IT, 7/78). Noyes later became a state legislator.

(49) Gary Carlson and Ralph Todd, economists working for the Omaha city government, found that 59% of the city's building owners would pay less if the property tax were two-rated LRT. See IT, 7/78.

(50) Buninyong (in rural Victoria) experienced a building boom – nearly five-fold – after it started taxing land values only instead of real-estate income (which was mainly a tax on buildings). The surrounding localities increased their construction and renovation also, but by less than half as much (source: A.B.S., as reported in *Progress,* 11/75, p. 11, also 11/76, p. 10; see IT, 11/78).

More studies are available.

Index

151

The Author

Steven Cord has devoted 54 years to the study of Henry George and land value taxation, and how it can solve current social problems.

His doctoral thesis, *Henry George: Dreamer or Realist?* was published by the University of Pennsylvania Press and is still in print by the Robert Schalkenbach Foundation; however, this book is more incisive. He has also published two other books.

He has been editor of a research newsletter for 30 years and has won four awards for research and writing, and has induced twenty localities (all cities except for a school district and a downtown business-improvement district) to tax land assessments more than building assessments. This gave him the opportunity to do 18 empirical studies, all of which show a construction and renovation increase within three years of a building-to-land shift in the local property tax.

Also, these localities *always* out-constructed and out-renovated nearby comparable localities that didn't make such a shift to land taxation, whenever such comparisons could be made.

Other highly qualified researchers have corroborated Cord's studies. His experience with economic reform is to be found in this book, explained as simply as possible. He explains how we can ensure the continuance of free enterprise and democracy via continuous prosperity for all.

Cord taught recent history and economics at Indiana University of Pennsylvania for nearly 25 years (from which he is now professor-emeritus). He has won four awards – two for research & writing and two for activism. He has also been the president of two nonprofit research organizations - the Henry George Foundation of America and the Center for the Study of Economics (which he founded in 1980).

He can be reached at stevencord2000@yahoo.com or at 10528 Cross Fox Lane, Columbia MD 21044.

Printed in the United States
26642LVS00005B/163-252